THE LONER GIRL IS AN EXISTENTIALIST

Self-Doubt, Irrational Feelings, and Internal Conflict

J. GUZMÁN

Loner Girl Press

For permissions and collaborations contact j@jguzman.space

You can connect with the author on Instagram @jguzmanwriter. Visit her website at jguzman.space and join her mailing list under the Contact tab.

to my cosmic overlord

everything is everything

I invoke you by all your names

for astrological purposes

Ana Ebtz
14 January 1991
8:42 a.m.
Lewiston, ID, USA

The Loner Girl is an Existentialist
(eBook version)
30 July 2020
7:31 a.m.
Boise, Idaho, USA

THE LONER GIRL IS AN
EXISTENTIALIST

✥

10 August 2009

I'm in Seattle! I've moved into the apartments with my teammates and had my first practice. It's preseason, so we don't
start school for about a month and I won't move into the
dorms until around that time. All the other freshman girls on
my team are going to live together in the dorms, but I chose
to room with two random people from school. I still haven't
met them.

Yesterday we moved in and had a barbecue with the whole
team, and it was fun and I know it'll get better, but I still feel
awkward and uncomfortable. I don't miss being home or in
Idaho, I just miss being alone or being able to do my own
thing, and having people that really understand me be there. I
don't have anything to say to these people!

I get anxious when I don't know how exactly I'm going to get
somewhere or what I'll need to bring with me or where to go.
Like yesterday we went shopping for food (our coach gives
us a ton of money for preseason food, it's crazy!) and I just

wanted to get a whole bunch of other stuff than my team-mates, and it's frustrating for me to have to comply with the majority's desires. I'd rather have my own stuff and work alone.

I felt like at practice I was running around with my head cut off. I did well in the mile (my time was 5:38), although I think the track isn't a full-sized track so that time is probably inaccurate. We also played in miniature games and I don't think I did well. Ugh. It's frustrating.

It's crazy to think that this is it; I am here to stay for a long time. I'm on my own and I dunno if I can handle that. It's scary! I'm kind of glad that I'm not rooming with any of my fellow soccer players in the dorms because they are not like me. I can't connect with them very well it seems like.

We had our second practice and I felt a bit better. Two prac-tices a day for two weeks, holy shit! We went to this little hole-in-the-wall place for dinner and ate eggs, hash browns, and french toast. It reminded me of the place I went to with Sawyer and Lacy after we went to the hot springs that one time.

I sat next to a senior on the team who is tiny and has bushy blonde hair and a squeaky mouse voice. She was super nice and told me about how when she was a freshman our coach asked her to say team prayer, since it's a Christian school. She was uncomfortable speaking in front of everyone so she awkwardly, quietly said prayer, and felt traumatized after-wards. That made me feel better because I just feel extremely uncomfortable and quiet right now. And there's no fucking way I will ever say prayer, that's for sure!

11 August 2009

Things have been getting better! I feel way more comfortable with the girls, the freshmen at least. Not as comfortable as I'd like, or as I could be with a person, I guess, but it's getting there. And it's only the second day of two-a-days, so I'd say my progress is good.

It's weird because all we do is soccer and I feel like I don't have a life other than that. I don't think I like that. I am excited for the day I'll have my own apartment and job and be able to buy my own food and have everything the way I want it, and be able to do fun things with friends that actually know me and want to do what I want to do.

I think I want to live in Seattle when I'm done with college. It's beautiful here and the variety of people and cultures is astounding. I can't believe I actually live here now; it's strange. I always felt like I'd be trapped in Boise for the rest of my life, so suddenly being somewhere really different and beautiful and lush and cloudy is hard to transition to.

For now I think I just need to stay in the moment and have fun living with my teammates and relax around other people and not get so anxious about everything. I wish I knew the surrounding area and had a bus schedule or car or something, but I guess that's all in time. I'll figure things out eventually, I suppose.

14 August 2009

Today was good. Things are getting much better, I can't even believe it. My touch on the ball is quickly improving and I'm getting progressively more comfortable playing on turf at such a fast pace.

The other day Bridgette and Mariah, two other freshmen,

3

both fit into these size large sweatpants, each in a separate leg, at the same time. It was hilarious!

Bridgette is this super tall girl from California. She always says, "Shut up!" instead of, like, "Oh my god!" It's funny. She's loud. Mariah is from Oregon, she has straight blonde hair and is very fast. She plays forward. They are both nice and I've started feeling less awkward around them, especially after we all laughed uncontrollably while they squeezed themselves into sweat-pant legs.

It's midnight and I'm bzzzing on coffee and wearing the same fuzzy grey sweats previously described, but in my own size. All the freshmen got them. I'm glad these things are getting better. I'm excited for school and the future and I hope I meet some interesting people.

16 August 2009

Today we had a day off because it's Sunday. We went downtown to Pike Place Market, and I bought a comic for one dollar for Sawyer for his birthday, which is in a few months. I just saw it and thought it was cool. But the guy sold it to me for less than it actually was, and when I asked him if there was tax he said, "Not for you!" I felt special.

Tomorrow's our last two-a-day practice and on Tuesday we go to Canada for a couple preseason games.

20 August 2009

We went to Canada and I roomed with one of the sophomores, Janet. I like her so it wasn't awkward. She has dark hair and lighter eyes and plays defense. She's nice and I think pretty religious as well, but not in the preachy, obnoxious way like most religious people.

That night in our game I didn't start, but I played 75% of the game and Chadwick, our coach, said he loved how I played, so that was very good. I didn't feel like I played especially well, but at least he's happy. Today we played another game and I started and played about 75% again, but I felt like I played badly. I couldn't breathe and it was hot and humid and terrible. We lost 1-0.

Also, Alexis, one of the other freshmen, and I had this intense conversation about crazy shit that we think about, and it made me feel sane and not alone in the universe. I like her a lot. She is half Hawaiian and really pretty, with long brown hair which is thin like mine, and big brown eyes and little teeth. She plays defense and everyone calls her Kan because that is her last name. We hung out a lot.

While walking around Vancouver with our team we found huge, old buildings that looked like they should be in Europe, and we decided which ones we would live in when we become rich and famous.

21 August 2009

I realized why I feel insane a lot of the time. I think it's because society says particular things are good and bad, and I just want to do whatever I want and disregard what people say or think, but people will always judge you! I don't want people to judge other people and say that what they are doing is bad or wrong or awkward, because they aren't in the same situation and probably don't know what's actually going on.

I don't want to think that what some people do is weird or

strange. I want to be fully receptive and tolerant and empathetic and understanding. And genuine! I'm worried that I'm judging people that do weird things when they are actually beautiful, artistic, misunderstood people, only because of society's creeping influence in the back of my mind that I can't get out, even though I know it's there.

I wish there were no drugs and that people would be different only because that's who they are. I wish people wouldn't take drugs because it makes them scary and they act strange and not rationally. It scares me because I can't connect with them and I don't know why they say certain things and nothing makes sense.

You know that it's not actually them when they are on drugs; it's their brain being warped. So it is like they are crazy at that moment. And I never know how to react to people! I want to think that they are unique and true, but if they are doing something weird on drugs it's not really them. As opposed to them doing something weird and being normal, like that's something they would do normally.* Ah, it's too complicated.

Something that's been scaring me is the fact that you can never truly connect with someone because you aren't in her mind and even if you are having a deep conversation, you never know if she is truly in agreement with everything you are saying. You don't know if secretly she is disagreeing with you about a certain thing and not telling you. I hate that.

I wish I knew what people were thinking so I could explain myself, because often people don't ask you questions when they disagree with you, they just stay silent and wonder why you said something. And criticize you. It makes me feel paranoid. I hate that I don't know if they understand my perception fully. It makes me feel alone and scared.

Things are just strange! Like sensing stimuli. Like hearing and feeling. Thinking. Thinking is so fucking weird it makes me so weird. Ugh, it's kind of beautiful but it scares me. Like how I know certain things are true because other things are true. Logic, doing math, writing an essay. Creepy and lovely at the same time. Or just writing this, even though the thought process is kind of scrambled. And how I know it's scrambled. And how I know I have to pee right now.

[*Ana: It actually *is* possible to be weird, on drugs, and genuine all at once. You can still be yourself on drugs. It depends on the drug *and* the person. Also, you'd need to define terms such as "drug," "normal," "weird," "true," and "crazy" to have a productive conversation about this. –J.]

23 August 2009

Yesterday was the longest day of my life. We got up at nine because practice was at ten, and the night before Kan and I stayed up till 2:30 a.m. talking, so we only got seven hours of sleep.

After practice the whole team went to Golden Gardens to ice bath in the ocean. It's this park by the beach and the water is freezing and beautifully, painfully soothing on sore muscles. We got Cuban food at this little pink shack by the beach and went to watch the guys' soccer team play while we ate.

When we finally got back to the apartments I took a fast shower, and then Kan, Hope, Mila, Sierra, and I went shopping at Goodwill, Urban Outfitters, and Red Light. I stole some measuring spoons from Urban Outfitters.

Hope, Mila, and Sierra are sophomores on my team. Hope and Mila are tall and skinny and are both from Colorado. Hope has curly brown hair and is tan and can run long distances faster than most. She has good endurance but doesn't play much during our games.

Mila has blonde, straight hair and I like her a lot. She kind of looks like Gwyneth Paltrow. She also has a thing with one of the guys on the soccer team who seems alternative and cool. I think his name is Trevor.

Sierra is from Utah, she plays center mid like me and is extremely good at soccer. I feel like our minds are similar, like she is awkward sometimes but funny at the same time and sort of on accident. I like her a lot because I feel like she gets it.

When we got home from shopping, we proceeded to get ready to go out to this fancy restaurant all dressed up. We got fast food first for dinner because we only wanted dessert at the fancy place. I didn't get anything though because I don't want the "freshman 15" and I figured I would just eat dessert for dinner.

When we got home from dinner we were doing nothing, and some of the guys on the soccer team came over to our apartment because they were very drunk. It was pretty funny. Kan and I stayed up till four in the morning talking to Max and Drake and Caleb.

Max is from Hawaii but he doesn't look Hawaiian as in the indigenous people of Hawaii. Drake is short and his nickname is Puka but Kan and I feel uncomfortable calling him that because it's like a weird pet name.

The other day we went to frozen yogurt and Caleb was there and he talked to me briefly about music. He is tall and a musician, I guess, or at least obsessed with music, and he kind of has a lisp or perhaps only talks funny. We went into this sweet music store that had everything, so last night he started talking to me about music while they were all drunk, and he showed me the band Bon Iver, which I am listening to right now. He fell asleep on our couch in this awkward position and we were making fun of him.

Drake drew a picture of me on the back of my soccer calendar. I felt special because I am interesting enough to make someone want to draw me.

26 August 2009

Today's Wednesday. We have a game tomorrow: the first one of the season that counts.

Last night Kan and I longboarded for a while with Mariah and Rick's longboards, and then hung out with some of the other guys on the soccer team.

It was decided that Mariah and Rick are kind of the same person, it's funny. They have similar personality and body types. Rick is not short but not tall, and he is really hairy, with a dark, curly beard and a shaggy mop of hair on his head.

The night before was basically the same; Dustin taught Kan and I how to longboard. He is short and from Washington, I think.

Sunday night we hung out with Max and Drake again. They are best friends, I guess, and since Kan and I are always hanging out now we pair up in a funny way. I always try to wink at Max because he always winks, but I can't without smiling. It's so hard. Him and Drake are such interesting people! They always talk about deep stuff and like to analyze everything. Drake is a psychology major, perhaps that is why.

Last night at nine we had a team meeting at our field. We

walked out to the center of it between lines of candles, and sat at tables with drinks and tall candles on them. We each stood and talked about our goals and one of the coaches filmed it. I was scared because I didn't know what to say at first, but after watching all the other girls talk I figured out what I wanted to say and I didn't mess up. My goals were short though, because I get nervous when talking in front of people.

We got gift bags from the seniors with candy and a shoelace to put in our right shoe to symbolize unity, and a black bracelet that says 'believe' on it. It was emotional, meaningful, inspirational! I hope we do really well this season. I want to be a part of something special, like winning the National Championship!

06 September 2009

Calvin, a sophomore on the guys' team, came over to our apartment and tried to cheer me up about last night. I played horrible in our game and it fucking sucked. I felt like no matter what I did I just couldn't get it together. I was so tired for some reason, and I felt like I couldn't keep running around in circles. Running around with my head cut off like a fucking stupid chicken. I kept passing to the other team, too. And Chadwick, our coach, yelled at me.

Anyway, Calvin and I played backgammon and I killed him. He is best friends with Trevor, the guy on the team that Mila has a thing with. Calvin is a ginger! With pale skin, but he has a nice body because he works so hard in soccer, and he is also really funny. He talks nonstop, kind of.

He wrote me a ridiculous note trying to make me feel better. I have a sneaking suspicion that he's in love with me because he always texts me and hugs me and jokingly calls me his girlfriend. It's very…interesting. He has red hair and I am not that into red-haired boys…

After having that awful game yesterday I'm nervous to play in California. It's stupid. I always think about how in a few years I'll never even remember how much yesterday sucked, and it just won't matter. It doesn't matter compared to my lifespan and being happy.

Soccer has been weird. It's a love/hate thing. I love scoring and playing well and winning, but I hate how much commitment it requires, and not being able to do certain things. It's worth it, I guess; it *is* enabling me to be here with friends (I do feel like now I am able to start calling these people my friends) and to get an education at a good school.

08 September 2009

This girl Tanya on my team was telling me the other day about how she hated everyone in high school and how her roommates were awful to her. I guess she went to some kind of boarding school where you live with classmates. But I thought, it's okay to do your own thing and not concern yourself with that many people, because your life should be what you want it to be.

It made me think about myself in the way I like to, like how I think about people in books and movies. It's about perspective and I think perspective is so important. We'd like to view ourselves a certain way. Perspective is what makes everyone insane, I think. Because everybody has different ways of viewing things and it's hard to really understand everything without getting confused.

We all have motives for doing things and when someone else watches you do something weird and they don't know the reason you're doing it, they don't understand you.

10 September 2009

Um, I am frustrated with myself because I am confused about who I am and how I am supposed to act around certain people, and I don't know how my face is supposed to look and what I'm supposed to say, and I feel like people can't take me seriously. All this is bouncing around in my head and I don't know who anyone is, especially by only looking at a person's Facebook, like my new dormmates, who I haven't met yet but I have their names and I looked them up.

Calvin asked me to go to sushi with him, and I don't know what to do because he makes me weird sometimes.

I've felt pretty annoying and immature lately. Especially yesterday, and it's because I don't know how to react so I just laugh or do something stupid. I feel misunderstood. I feel way too aware of myself and I wish I'd do or be something interesting. Or come up with something really unique.

Oh, and also I'm getting extremely irritated with living with all of these people. I need to be alone or with only one person. Aahhh.

11 September 2009

We had a game today and won. Josie, a senior, scored all our goals. I had a breakaway and missed. It sucked, but I bet it looked a lot closer to the people in the stands than it actually was.

When we got back from the game Max, Drake, and Ronan

were sitting in our apartment wearing all my hats and listening to our music. Assholes broke in through the balcony. Now that I think about it, Ronan still has one of my hats! He is from Portland and is an interesting person. He plays forward and is super fast. I like him because he wears cool clothes and is different. His style could probably be classified as "alternative," which I like a lot.

Later, after I took a shower, I played backgammon with Max and made coffee, and Kan made cookies. Such good vibes!

We move into the dorms in a couple of days, it's crazy. I met one of my roommates in person today. It was so random, she was at orientation and I happened to be standing on the right corner of the right street at the exact time she walked by. We both sort of recognized each other because we found each other on Facebook. What are the odds? She seemed nice, and her outfit was great! I hope she's cool.

15 September 2009

I was thinking about how a person can understand more things about herself if she is around other people and notices the way they do things. It's interesting to view how other people organize their room and to observe the artifacts they have collected, and to listen to the music they have.

Lately I've been trying hard to be confident about how I do things, and what I own, and to not question myself or wonder if I should do something the way everyone else is doing it. I'm going to do things the way I first imagined doing them.

We finally moved into the dorms a couple days ago. Today I fell asleep on the floor in the lobby of Kan's dorm while she played the piano. She is living in the dorms at the bottom of the hill on campus, and I'm living in the dorms at the top of the hill.

18 September 2009

I just wanted to say that Kan has been making me so weird lately. Like, she is super bossy sometimes and tries to control everything. Today I was texting Calvin at breakfast, and she was like, "Stop texting him, you are totally leading him on, it's stupid! You text nonstop!"

It really pissed me off because I've told him that I don't love him, that I don't feel exactly the same way towards him, so I am not leading him on, sorry! Also, I do not text him nonstop, like, for example, I haven't texted him since breakfast. And I can text him nonstop anyway if I wanted to; it's my fucking life. I can be friends with whoever the fuck I want.

It's like she can't handle me talking to boys. It's the weirdest, most irritating situation ever! Also, she was texting Drake yesterday when I was texting Calvin, so she's being a huge hypocrite! She texts him a lot, so why can't I be friends with Calvin and text him? Ah, it's been making me angry. She is very controlling.

Something I noticed about her that irritates me is that she is very full of herself. Like, she always talks about how her hair is pretty, and how she is so good at soccer, and how she didn't have that many guy friends because they all ended up liking her and having crushes on her, and how she has such good skin, and how she's really tan, and how she rarely has to shave because her hair doesn't grow, and oh my god it gets extremely annoying! So I'm frustrated with her right now.

I just got intensely angry today (in my mind) when she told

me to stop texting Calvin. I don't even know why. It was like she was acting as if she had authority over me and was reprimanding me for being an idiot. I hate when I become good friends with someone and then they start doing weird shit like that, like telling you what you are doing is stupid or bad, or telling you how to act.

This is why I hate people. And I hate the fact that I probably have done this, or still do it to friends that I have had or still have. I'm a hypocrite only because I'm human, and I despise this fact. Ugh.

Anyway, all the freshmen on the soccer teams have settled into dorm life. It's totally fine. My roommates don't move in for another few days, so I got first pick of everything and have the room all to myself. It's relaxing having a space to be alone.

23 September 2009

Yesterday practice was hot and tiring and the worst thing ever. But I finished my book later so I felt accomplished.

I hung out with Kan in her dorm, and Drake came over and we hung out with him. I think they have a thing, sort of, or at least they have crushes on each other and won't say. I dunno, they haven't hooked up or anything.

Later I went to Calvin's and watched *I Love You, Man* with him and Mila and Trevor, and it was fun. I wore his Snuggie. Actually, we wore it together, at the same time. Haha.

Today I was reading the magazine *Cosmopolitan* and it put me in this crazy irritated mood, because it's all bullshit. It made me think about how much I hate people, and then I felt like no one likes me and I have no friends and I hate how I act around people. A lot of the time I don't give a fuck, but other times it really bothers me.

Tomorrow my roommates move in and I'm probably not going to get any sleep because I bet you anything they'll come barging in here at like seven a.m. and I'll want to kill myself. Not that I don't already.

24 September 2009

Okay, I do not know who I am at all lately. It seriously is getting bad. Today practice was all right. Afterwards a few of us freshmen went to this stupid freshman orientation thing where the president of the university talked and it was boring as fuck. Then we ate at this place in the center of campus and later went to the cafeteria, and I was in a stupid mood.

I put coffee in Calvin's cereal because he put cereal in my coffee, and I just felt very angry and irritated, as well as irritating to other people. Then I went back to the dorms and took a shower and went to another freshman thing, and I met a couple of people in my Japanese class.

My Japanese class is like a freshman introduction to college class. There were a ton of classes to choose from, but I chose the Japanese one because I think that culture is interesting and I don't know anything about it. And I totally want to learn about manga and anime and shit like that. I don't think it's a language class, necessarily; it should be more about the culture and customs and maybe a tiny bit about the language.

Then there was a meeting in my dorm for my floor, and a root beer keg party behind the gym, which was stupid. I ended up ditching that and going to bubble tea with Calvin because he asked me. I dunno what the deal with him is anyway, it's weird. We hang out a lot, sort of. At least we did when we were living in the apartments. But we are completely opposite; I don't know why he likes me! And I don't think I like him that much, anyway.

My roommates moved in today. It was okay. Their names are Lillian and Natalie. Only Lillian is here right now because Natalie had to go to a wedding or something. Lillian is Mexican and tiny and nice, and Natalie has long blonde hair and is obsessed with *Star Wars* and a lot of other weird stuff, like children's shows. I feel really uncomfortable around them.

I have been so confused about myself. I feel weird and I don't know how to react to people and it's making me crazy. Then, when I do react in a certain way, I immediately regret it and feel like a fool, and I hate that about myself. I don't want to hate myself but I am just so fucking awkward and incapable of interacting with people and it sucks so bad.

25 September 2009

Kan and I talked today about how we don't know who we are and how we think we are insane and weird shit like that. It was comforting knowing that I'm not alone.

28 September 2009

Today was the first day of school! It was totally fine. My Japanese class is tiny and I think the people in it are nice but I'm not sure yet. Right after that I had Logic, which was super interesting and it made a lot of sense to me, so I hope it's always like that. I also went to my Middle Ages class. Incredibly boring. I regret taking that class and it's the first day of school. Shit.

29 September 2009

Oh, my god. Last night I was texting Calvin and I asked him why he likes me and this is what he texted me:

"Number one I think that you are gorgeous and to go with that you don't care what anyone thinks or need to impress anyone. You're simple and make me want to hang out with you all the time. You're really cute when you laugh and even cuter when you beat me in games. You like to joke around and fake wrestle with me when you know you will lose, but do it so you can flirt anyway. And my favorite thing is that you like to Snuggie with me and no matter how many times you say it, you definitely wanted to hold my hand when we were walking yesterday."

Haha! Isn't that cute?

02 October 2009

Today's Friday. Yesterday I didn't have class so I did all my homework in the university library with Calvin. He brought me a coffee, it was awesome. I also talked to both my parents on the phone because they are coming to our game tomorrow.

Calvin's making me weird because he acts like we're going out sometimes and I don't want him to. It's creepy a tiny bit. I haven't hung out with the other guys on the soccer team in *forever*, it's sad. I don't want them all to think we're dating or something.

Right now I'm really anxious because this morning wasn't the greatest. It was raining a lot and I slid onto one knee when walking down the hill, and my knee was bleeding everywhere in class.

My Japanese class was boring as fuck because these stupid kids kept asking irrelevant questions so we didn't have time for origami. Then Logic was longer than it should have been so the cafeteria line was a mile long when I finally got there, so I just came back to my dorm to eat.

I've been thinking about the whole Calvin thing and who I am and what I'm going to do with my life and if I'll have enough money to live when I'm older and if I'll get a job and if I'm smart enough for my classes, and it's freaking me out. It's bad. I was in such a bad mood last night because I was immersed in all that shit.

Everything seems futile and hopeless. Now I have to go to my Middle Ages class, which is going to be fucking awful and I'll probably fall down the hill again.

05 October 2009

I told Calvin how I feel about him, and how I don't want to be involved with someone seriously because commitment freaks me out, and how I don't like him as much as he likes me. I think we have it all cleared up. I said I didn't want to lead him on but I like hanging out with him because he's hilarious.

We lost our game the other day. I played though, and my parents were there, so it was all right.

06 October 2009

Last night I went over to Calvin's apartment to do my home-work and to get my phone since I left it over there, and I ended up sleeping over, in his bed with him. We got up in the middle of the night and played backgammon and couldn't sleep. So much for not leading him on.

Today we won our game 1-0. I only played for 20 minutes. Not at all in the second half. I don't know why. After that a few people on both the men's and women's soccer teams went to bubble tea, and I don't know why I went because I didn't buy anything.

I'm going to bed, I don't know what else to say. I feel weird and depressed. There's nothing to do. I don't like anything anymore. I can't play soccer how I used to be able to play. There's a barrier blocking me and I can't get past it.

I don't feel like a real person. I feel like a stranger to myself. I don't get a lot of sleep, but perhaps that's a good thing. I never know if I'm being immature or if people of all ages act the way I do sometimes. I don't want to lose my childhood mentally.

I don't know what to do with myself.

09 October 2009

Today I went to this thrift store that's exactly like one in Boise except with a different name. Calvin drove me there because he wanted to go. I stole two bracelets, one is made with red dice. Calvin got the same one except his is black. The other is Asian-looking and says, "We are the hero of our own story," which felt true and real to me. It was five dollars so I felt kickass badass stealing it.

I slept over at Calvin's apartment last night after freshman orientation activities, and I kissed him. We made out, actually. For the first time. It was fun, I guess. He doesn't make me feel creepy like Davis did that one night. I'm embarrassed because I think everyone knows because he has a big mouth and Trevor said he heard us kissing, since they sleep in the same room.

I dunno how I feel, because I like Calvin, and I like kissing and cuddling with him and spending the night, because all those things are fun. But I don't want to be his girlfriend because I want to be able to do those things with other boys, too, if the situation ever arose.

But I don't want to hurt him, you know? Because I obviously wouldn't want to cheat on him, and if we were dating then I couldn't do anything with other guys and I know that I would probably want to. Especially because I haven't really dated at all or been with that many guys and I want to experience more.

I just feel super shallow maybe, because what if I meet another, cuter guy? I know that Calvin and I don't have the same personalities, and he's not someone I want to be with for the rest of my life, so why does there have to be any commitment? I guess I feel like after college I'm going to be an adult and it would be closer to marriage, and that freaks me out. I never want to get married! I guess I shouldn't worry about it. Sawyer is six years older than me and has a thing with Lacy, and they aren't getting married! Yet, at least.

I feel like whenever a guy likes me, he likes me way too much and wants to be with me forever. Like sophomore year in high school, Eli and I would never have broken up if I didn't end it. And Davis liked me for three fucking years, which he told me when we were drunk, and asked me (also when we were drunk) if I was going to meet someone in college that I'd ditch him for. What the fuck!?

I'm a free spirit and I don't like to be held down! I want to be able to do whatever the fuck I want, when I want. I worry way too fucking much, it's ridiculous. I need to slow down and live in this moment and open my eyes to how beautiful Seattle is, and realize that I'm in college and there are nice people and interesting things to learn, and that I'm a real person and I do fucked up things and make mistakes, and bad things happen to me and good things happen to me.

When I get too frustrated I cry a little, like on the soccer field, but not enough for anyone to notice. I think I'm ugly, but a few people think I'm pretty, and a boy told me I was a good kisser last night when I slept in his bed, and I told him I didn't know if I wanted him to kiss me and that I confuse myself, but then our lips touched anyway.

I don't know how my face looks when I talk to people, and often I look really mad when I'm perfectly fine. I don't know what's right and what's wrong, because there are so many perspectives. I want to be into Buddhism because it seems right, being good to people, being wise, but at the same time I sometimes want to do bad things like steal bracelets from thrift stores and be an asshole to the people around me.

I feel as if I'm the only one who understands these things! That's why people frustrate me and make me angry. But I *do* realize that other people feel the same and feel misunderstood, and this is when I start to hate myself because I want to know them like I wish people knew me. I want to be who I wish people would be to me, but I just end up avoiding them. I have social anxiety and certain situations make me nervous, like shopping in a crowded grocery store.

Sometimes I wish I didn't exist because things are futile and tedious and complicated, and it really sucks sometimes. But other times I know things are magical, like when the sun strikes the trees and the leaves are turning yellow and red, and when the sky gets dark and purple-blue bruised. Or how you feel when you hear the rain and listen to it somewhere where you won't get wet.

I can understand how these things are important. A lot of the time I wish I could be really good at something, and a lot of the time there's something around me whispering that I'll do something influential, but it's only a feeling. Most of the time I can't decide if I want to be somebody, or if I want to be kept a secret and do random things like give plasma and spend the money earned on coffee and other things you can't steal.

I want something bad to happen to me, just so I can feel it. I want to know how far I can go. I want someone to put a gun to my head so I can tell them to pull the trigger because I'm not afraid to die. And I don't want that to be a lie! I want to say things I mean. I say things I don't mean sometimes and I loathe this.

I hate those awkward conversations you have with people when you first meet and there's nothing to say, because there's an infinite amount of things you don't know about them, but where do you even start? It makes me so anxious. I dunno if people like me and I dunno if I'd be my friend if I weren't me. Sometimes I don't give a fuck and other times I really, really care.

11 October 2009

Yesterday I woke up and felt a tad bit sick because my throat was sore and my whole body felt kind of weird, like an indescribable weird, like how you can't describe how it is to be high to someone that's never smoked mota.

Sierra and I went to Uwajimaya, the Asian grocery store, and it was the coolest place ever! I felt like I was in Japan. I couldn't read anything because it was all in Japanese and all their stuff is interesting and cutely decorated. I bought a manga I'm supposed to read for my Japanese class.

Right now I'm drinking tea and listening to the band Phoenix and sort of texting Calvin, who is still in love with me. I'm at Starbucks on Queen Anne hill. I saw Ari, a junior on my team, at a drug store and we talked for a little while, and I felt fucking awkward and insane and it sucked because I didn't know what to say to her.

I could tell my face got really red, and all I could think about was how she would react to how I couldn't talk right. It's hard to talk to people when all you can think about is what they are thinking.

Today wasn't amazing, but it's been all right. It felt nice to walk around in the sun and see the leaves turning yellow, and I felt like a real person. I dunno what it is, but college doesn't make me feel real like I thought it would. Maybe it's because everyone's Christian at my school and they're all my age and being around people my age makes me nervous. And homework makes me nervous and weird. I think when things make me anxious I don't feel real. Ahhh, this is making me crazy. I'm real, I swear I am, why can't I feel it?*

[*Ana: You don't feel real because you're not independent and your life is subject to other people's rules, which will always make you feel trapped and inhibited. You felt trapped living at home with your parents and being stuck in high school. Now you feel trapped by soccer's dictating how you live your life and everyone's close-minded perception that Christianity is Truth. You can see these themes of imprisonment reflected in Saturn's strong emphasis in your natal chart, as well as your heavy 12th house placements. –J.]

Yesterday when I was walking around by Queen Anne I found this graveyard that I had never been to before. There is this beautiful view, and it was lovely just standing there, pretending nothing existed but my eyes and the hills and trees and cars and bridge, and how in the graveyard nothing moved, and I could stand there breathless with no sounds anywhere and the chilly air surrounding me.

When I got back to school Natalie and I went to dinner and there were no forks, as usual. I feel lost right now. I don't even know how I feel, but it's not good.

Today I had classes and they were fine. In my Middle Ages class I talked to a cute boy. His name is Sam. He has gauges in his ears and tattoos. The girl next to me said he was staring at me. He told me he said hi to me in the cafeteria, but I guess I didn't hear because I don't remember that at all. I have a small crush on him, and when I realized this I also realized that I don't want to be seriously involved with Calvin. I mean, I already knew, but I realized I needed to tell him. And be serious about it.

I went to the cafeteria with Kan before practice today, and she said Drake told her about me and Calvin making out, and that made me so mad that Calvin told everybody. I'm a private person, and when I'm vulnerable with another person it hurts when they share that moment with everyone else!

So that put me in a bad mood. Then practice sucked; I still can't play soccer. I feel like it's getting worse. I can't figure out why I can't figure out my touch on the ball! Now I'm in my dorm room. I told Calvin everything through texting and it's been established that we're friends with benefits. Which will still probably turn out bad, but whatever. Ugh.

After practice yesterday I went to Calvin's and was in a bad mood and ate pizza and then I played their Nintendo, and it put me in the best mood ever! It was the only thing good that happened to me all day. I am the best at Mario, so it felt really good to play. It also reminded me of home.

I slept over in Calvin's bed, and then this morning Mila drove me back to my dorm so I could get ready for our game, which was an away game.

I forgot to bring my long-sleeve jersey so Chadwick was pissed at me because as a team we have to all wear the same outfit. Mariah forgot hers, too, so Chadwick wouldn't let her start (she usually starts), which I think is childish and vindictive of him.

I only played in the game for, like, ten minutes. It was stupid. It sucks; I feel like every game I'm playing less and less. It sucks because I need time to get used to myself, and if I don't play then I won't be able to figure myself out. Chadwick doesn't say why I'm not playing very much, but I have a strong feeling that he's doing it on purpose to make a point, which I cannot figure out.

I just became kinda depressed because I was looking at Mila's Facebook profile, and she had all these pics of her and the other sophomores doing fun things, like going to a pumpkin patch and making Halloween sugar cookies. I feel like I have no friends to do things like that with, and no one likes me, and it's an awful feeling.

I'm just super fucking awkward with people, and I noticed that I'm that way with Cameron a lot. She is a sophomore on the team and plays center mid like me, and the one that had mota on my recruiting trip. I think she is really cool, but she probably hates me because I'm stupid and annoying and suck at soccer.

15 October 2009

I hope I can make it through practice without wanting to kill myself. I would consider it a huge psychological feat.

18 October 2009

We had a game in Boise. It went well, I guess. I played a lot, but only with all the second string players that don't start, so I was in a bad mood. We won 7-0 though. Then I went home with my parents and I got to see Jenna. My aunt and uncle on Dad's side were there as well. I got to take a shower before my parents took me to the airport for Seattle.

It was strange being home. I haven't been there in what felt like forever. On the plane ride back I sat next to Mila, and we had this serious conversation about depression and insecurity and life, and it was nice. I think she is one of the most interesting people ever because she's gone through a lot of hard stuff. I look up to her.

She told me that she wanted to kill herself in high school and that her preferred method was to hang herself. It's crazy because now she seems really happy and cares a lot about other people, and I can't imagine her wanting to hang herself in high school, or ever. I guess it gives me this weird hope. I think it makes me feel like things are okay.

19 October 2009

Today was perhaps one of the best days I've had in a real

27

long time. At practice I played better than I have in forever. Chadwick told me I played well. I decided that I've been playing like I'm scared or like I have no confidence, and I want to change that very badly, so I'm going to.

It feels important that I recognized this in myself and that I'm going to work to change it. I feel like that's something I've never done before: realized something bad about myself, accepted it, and decided to change it.

23 October 2009

Right now I'm in my hotel room in LA. We are here for a game. Mila is my roommate! Roomies! We just got back from practice and our game is tomorrow. At breakfast I sat by Calvin and Trevor and Mila, because the guys are at our same hotel.

Calvin came up to my room and we kissed on the balcony. The Sam kid from my Middle Ages class added me on Facebook, asked for my phone number, and started texting me, and I get the weirdest vibes from him now. I think it's possible he is super religious.

24 October 2009

The insanely unfathomable amount of people in the world is the source of all my despair. Because there's no use trying to accomplish anything since there's always going to be someone better than you. How can you be happy if everything you do is one-upped by someone else, often your friends?

I always feel like I'm not good enough, and I hate this feeling. It sucks. Maybe this is why I'm never satisfied, because there's always something better. Same with guys! How could I ever be happy with one person when I know there's someone better out there? This is why I'll never get married. I don't understand why I feel this way. It makes me unhappy, always.

I've been trying to study for my Middle Ages class, but it just isn't working. I can't concentrate. I can't do history, it's fucking boring. Why did I sign up for this class? Midterm on Monday, I'm going to fail.

We went to the guys' game last night. They lost, unfortunately, but they played well. There was this one time where Calvin fell and was on his back, and then he jumped back onto his feet like a ninja, it was fucking hilarious! I seriously could not stifle my laughter.

We ate dinner at Ari's house because she's from California and her house is fairly close to our hotel. The food was delicious. But I still hate food! I feel trapped in my body. And I feel fat all the time.

I keep thinking that I wouldn't like myself if I weren't me. Or rather, if there were two of me we would hate each other because we would compete. I feel like I secretly make everything into a competition to see who's better. Like with Kan. But, I dunno, I don't do that with Mila or Cameron, or any of the older girls.

Maybe because Kan and I are so close, basically like sisters. Although I don't have a real sister so I don't even know what that would feel like. Maybe I feel like I wouldn't like myself because I feel misunderstood a lot and I can understand how people must view me since they don't know what goes on in my brain. There, that's settled.

27 October 2009

We are back from California. We lost our game and I played for literally 20 minutes.

Today I didn't have class so I slept over at Calvin's last night, and when I woke up he handed me this bouquet of flowers and said, "I found these on the side of the road and I thought I should give them to you." Shuffled his feet and laughed a bit. It was funny, a little cute.

But then all day he was in a pissy mood because he's confused about what I want, which is no attachment, and he wants me to be his girlfriend and he doesn't know what to do. And now I don't know what to do.

Today I bought some pink hair dye and bleach for my hair and put a fake penguin tattoo on my arm.

30 October 2009

We tied our home game and I only played for ten minutes in the second overtime. And I don't know why. Chadwick is fucking insane. It was brutally cold, and Mila and I talked while we were on the bench together. It was fun, we talked about how good at soccer we are that we sit on the bench all game.

Today was my group's turn for "cadres" for my Japanese class, which is basically where the class splits into groups and hangs out with the teacher for a little bit to talk and ask questions. Awkward. My group met in our teacher's office and had nothing to talk about so I didn't say anything. The other people in my group talked about high school and shared stories, and I just sat there silently. I fucking hated high school so I obviously had no funny or interesting things to say about that.

It was awkward because our teacher's office is small and cluttered, and we sat around this tiny circular table and had no room. I was late to Logic because our Japanese teacher never told us what time it was while we were in our cadre. He's kind of strange. He didn't really say anything during our cadre, either.

Today at practice we have to wear costumes for Halloween. I'm going to be Hello Kitty because I adore her. We are also driving to Oregon after practice because we have a game there.

Important things, vibrations:

Man in evil bunny costume on the street corner, sitting next to Sam and seeing him watch me from the corner of my eye, finding great meaning in particular words, buying food at Whole Foods Market, latching on to something and believing in it just to believe in something, realizing I don't trust anyone, I can't trust anyone, wanting to ask my Japanese teacher a million questions about Buddhism and Japan, professors' offices, girl at Whole Foods with bunny outfit and face painting,

nihilism and rejecting society, weird outfits, wanting to take pills for anxiety because I can't talk to anyone, pigtails for Hello Kitty costume, trying so fucking hard, trying to change something I hate about myself, failing, getting sudden vibes that everything is okay, realizing that people believe in something you don't, and strongly, and for good reason, realizing you're good at something, wanting to be Trevor because he is a guy with good style and music abilities and confidence, street lamps at night, showing someone something personal, knowing something you did or made is cool, night, forests and mist, thinking I'm not mentally strong and hating it and wanting to change it, and having other people know this and use it against me, getting really fed up with things and fighting back, throwing it all away, giving everything up and having nothing to lose, not knowing if I'm hungry so not eating, infinity, fighting your body and mind,

knowing people don't understand you even when they think they do and feeling bad about it and not knowing what to do, not knowing what you want, wanting to know *everything* about a certain person, when the things I say scare Calvin because he doesn't understand my depression, reading about other people's lives and wondering why your life can't be like that but when it is at the same time - you have problems just like the people in the books, internal conflict,

how people's opinions of you seem important when they're *not*, asking people what they are thinking, wanting to be the clouds and the ocean and the trees and the atmosphere, wanting certain moments to never end, understanding how fast time is slipping away, reacting to certain situations quickly and without thinking, and then later thinking about it and liking how you reacted, wanting pain in order to feel something, irrational fear, self-control,

embracing your humanity while at the same time wanting to rip it apart, tear it off like old clothes, feeling weak when you have to rely on someone else in order to accomplish something or needing other people's help, especially for matters concerning mental health, the lyrics to Björk's song "Jóga"

02 November 2009

32

I am stressed for no reason. I slept at Calvin's last night. I don't think I like him because yesterday we went to the grocery store and I noticed that we never talk about anything serious. Every time I try to talk seriously he'll just say something annoying or irrelevant or say, "shut up." He doesn't know who I am, but he thinks he does and it's frustrating and irritating. He never asks about me, either, about who I am or my past. So I don't want to be around him for a while.

I started in our game. I don't know why I did, and I don't think I did terribly, but I did only play for, like, 15 minutes. I can't figure out why Chadwick does that - starts me but then after 15 minutes I stop and don't play for the rest of the game. It doesn't make any sense. I feel like he is punishing me for something I did and I don't know what it is. It's probably just me playing in this weird vague funk that I can't get out of. It's annoying.

On the drive to Oregon Chadwick was questioning Lia really hard about why she didn't dress up in a costume for Halloween practice. She is another freshman on the team that is super religious. She told Chadwick that Halloween is kind of against her religion, or at least she doesn't feel comfortable celebrating it, and Chadwick would *not* let it go.

He kept prying and prying and you could tell she didn't want to talk about it, and it was extremely uncomfortable being in the car while he did that to her. You could tell he was pissed about her not dressing up since it is a team tradition, but it was strange because it doesn't even matter! It's not like she refused to go to practice or something. But he interrogated her about it anyway.

I mean, I personally think people that don't celebrate Halloween because of their religion are weird as fuck, mainly because I think super religious people in general are weird as fuck, but I don't really care about it. Like, let them do whatever they want, it's not a big deal. Other people not celebrating Halloween does not affect me at all, so it was weird seeing how obviously angry Chadwick was about it. He is always trying to get into everyone's business, I fucking hate it.

On Halloween I didn't go trick-or-treating even though I wanted candy. Instead, Kan and I played Nintendo at the guys' apartment all night and also did our homework. All the guys went to parties and got drunk. We couldn't because we aren't allowed to drink during soccer season. It kind of sucks.*

Drake dressed up in my jean skirt and over-the-knee socks and wore my lipstick and a long blonde wig and looked absolutely ridiculous. He got hammered and threw up all night. I felt bad for him.

[*Ana: You know, sometimes rules are meant to be broken. –J.]

03 November 2009

I didn't hang out with Calvin at all yesterday, and I slept in my own bed last night, and I think that's good. Real good. Because I've been getting way too attached when I don't even like him that much.

I've started acting differently. Like, before school when we were living in the apartments, I would do my own thing and be mean to him sometimes and hang out with Max and Drake more. Now I've been more clingy, like hanging out all the time and always going over there and texting him without him texting me first. I don't know why.

I've been acting like an annoying girlfriend and I hate that. So I'm severing the ties, kind of. Not in a harsh way because he has a car and an apartment and Nintendo. Haha...And anyway, I still do want to be friends!

I have another thing to say. Yesterday at practice we had a team talk about trust. And how we don't have any, kind of. Like, we are not always sure if our teammates will be there for us at all moments on the field. I guess what I need to do is quit worrying about myself and my playing time, and only focus on working as hard as I can for my teammates. Just keep running; not for my own benefit, but so I can stop the person that beat our captain, or whoever, so that her effort wasn't for nothing. This is what I'm going to try to do.

All this talk about trust and being more vulnerable with each other made me feel really uncomfortable. Because I feel like I can't trust anyone a lot of the time, and I don't like being vulnerable with people because of this. And anyway, I don't think only having that talk can generate trust; it doesn't work like that. Also, I am just fucking bad at communicating my emotions to people, bad at communicating in general.

I don't know what the fuck's wrong with me.*(1) Probably part of it is me not trusting anyone, and part of it is that I'm shy and I don't know how to open up without feeling like a dumbass or crying. I don't know why I can't trust people. I think it's only because I know that people are human; they make mistakes and can hurt you all the time, even if it's on accident.

People tell other people secrets they should have kept, *all the time*! This makes me not want to tell anyone anything, ever. Sometimes your best friends treat you like shit, and then when I find someone I actually care about I don't want to give them the opportunity to hurt me, so I don't want to be vulnerable with them. But that's the only way to get close to someone!

Also, I hate when people you just meet try to pry into you, like the Sam kid in my Middle Ages class. He got into my business too fast and I don't even like him at all I realized. Maybe if he were, like, super hot I would feel differently. I mean, he is good looking but his vibes are weird and very Jesusy. I realized this yesterday. I'm pretty sure he's a player. I bet he talks to a million girls and they think they are special when in reality he does it to everyone. So I don't trust him one bit.

This diary is the sole owner, besides myself, of all the vulnerability and emotion and trust that is a part of me. No one else has delved this deep within me. I guess you could say I'm my own best friend. I dunno how I feel about this.

I want to publish my diaries. I think that'd be the ultimate enlightenment. Baring your whole fucking soul, throwing it all away. I guess it's kind of depressing, knowing that no one else knows me completely. People don't understand, and that sounds emo but it's true.

Meeting people is hard, too, because I just keep thinking about how complex I feel, and how fucking long it would take someone to actually know who I am. And that's hard.

I feel like if I could get a second opinion on this diary, like when you get a second opinion on a paper you wrote and they edit it and tell you what they think in their own words, and tell you how they interpreted it, I might better be able to understand who I am.*(2) For example, they could point out things that happen often and be like, "See, you have an eating disorder," or, "See, you are paranoid and anxious," or, "See, you have obsessive compulsive disorder!" But I don't know if that'll ever happen. It would be helpful, though.

Oh! I have another thing to say. I don't like doing things unless I know that they're absolutely going to work out. I have no faith. It's hard for me to believe in something when I don't know that it for sure will work out, and I think this is a problem. I need to forget about whether things will succeed.

I feel like I see things as being the end of the world if I don't make them work out. I need to realize that I'm a real person and I can make mistakes and fuck things up and do things wrong. I just don't want to be a slacker, or not be genuine, or think I'm a certain way and be lying to myself about it and not know who I truly am.

I need to start acting how I really am to people, and not being insecure about myself and be confident. I need to realize that soccer isn't my whole life, and neither is school, but they are both important.

[*(1) Ana: Nothing's "wrong" with you. What you're feeling is probably big Capricorn 12th house energy. You've got the Sun, Moon, Mercury, Uranus, Neptune, Saturn, and the North Node here. Wow, no wonder you think you're insane.

*(2): You won't know this for quite some time, but what you truly want is to be an astrological case study. You want someone to use you as an example to demonstrate the veracity of astrology's symbolic, archetypal system. You want someone well-versed in the language of time to explain to you astrological concepts and techniques, using your own beingness as the raw data.

You want to be consumed by metaphysical magic, you want to feel, to see, to understand the interconnectedness of Everything. You want to be the secret mirror, the elusive knower of hidden things. You want to hold cosmic power in your hands, in your mind, in the white Light at your center. You want to be One with All. Astrology can show you the way. –J.]

04 November 2009

Kailey, a junior on my team, told me that Chadwick told her that Mark (the guys' soccer coach) told him that Calvin likes me. Hahaha. So that means that Calvin told his fucking coach about me. What a freak!

Oh, we also had a talk about this thing going on between us and how we don't want it to escalate into what Mila and Trevor are doing, because someone's going to get hurt. And what Mila and Trevor are doing is basically dating but not defining themselves. They are acting exclusive but are not technically exclusive. If one of them hooked up with another person it would be bad because they are totally exclusive even though they pretend they aren't...I dunno, it's weird.

Calvin and I kind of figured things out, but not really. I told him it bothered me how he wasn't listening to me the other day at the grocery store and telling me to shut up or just cutting me off, and that was good. It worked, I guess. I think he'll be more serious now.

I'm still trying to not be attached. I find myself wanting to be around him or with him, but I don't know if this is because I actually like him, or if it's because I like the vibes I get from his apartment and roommates, and I'm so used to being around him that his presence is vaguely comforting. Ugh.

08 November 2009

Lately I've been playing a lot of Nintendo. Kan and I always play Mario. On Friday we were playing Mario and no one could get past level 7-2, and finally after, like, an hour, I beat it and freaked out and was really loud and annoying. Haha.

09 November 2009

I got a 94% on my Logic exam. Boo fucking yah.

10 November 2009

Emotionally purging. I don't know what I'm supposed to do. I feel trapped in the human form. I feel things. I'm made to have emotions and it would be much simpler without them. I think that in Buddhism, if you become enlightened, you rise above those emotions, that strange humanity. Or at least not let them affect you so much.

In the book I have to read for my Middle Ages class, *Revelations of Divine Love*, it keeps talking about how when you get to heaven you'll have eternal happiness and the greatest possible joy. I don't think this is right. I think you should either feel all emotions, or none. You can't just feel joy and bliss all the fucking time, for the rest of eternity. It seems wrong to me.

The Buddhist emptiness thing seems much better. Righter, truer. Even if I do think that's truer, I'm still stuck with uncertainty because how can I know for sure? I'm still stuck with these fucking feelings, these irrational feelings, like that other people don't love me or that I'm completely alone inside my own mind, or confusion about what love is anyway.

Or being kind of upset that Calvin was talking to and maybe flirting with some girl the other day when I *know* that we're just friends (…with benefits?) and that I honestly do not want

39

to be with him. I wonder if I'm upset that he's not still obsessed with me because I'm selfish and I want everyone to like me. Ugh, I don't know anything.

13 November 2009

Yesterday we were in San Diego for the first round of the final tournament, and we fucking lost. We are out. I cannot believe it. I didn't play at all. Oh well, I'm glad it's over and I don't have to deal with Chadwick.

I roomed with Aubry, who has short blonde hair like me, and Sierra. We watched this ridiculous movie called *Firecracker*. It was so bad. It was hilarious though, only because it was awful and they did the strangest shit. Like, for example, it kept changing from black and white to color, and oh my god. I can't even explain.

Later Kan and Mariah and I watched *Donnie Darko*, and I am in love with Jake Gyllenhal after that. He is seriously super sexy. For some reason I'm attracted to the dark and slightly insane, or at least troubled.

Last night after we lost I got drunk with some of the sophomores and juniors, and it was the best thing ever! We played King's Cup and then threw cereal at each other and sat in the hot tub. I went to bed at 4:30 a.m. I was the only freshman, too, so I felt privileged.

Molly, a junior who is our goalie, said that now that I'm a sophomore (in soccer season terms) she can be nice to me. It was stupid, because people like her are the reason our team doesn't have unity or trust. She and her friend Becky on the team never welcomed us as freshmen. They were always aloof and wouldn't really talk to us, but now that I'm not a

40

freshman they can act like we belong on the team. It's rude and doesn't make any sense.

I'm alone in my dorm room right now because Natalie and Lillian both went home for the weekend. They both live in Washington, fairly close to Seattle, so they go home for the weekends sometimes.

Kan and I made a list of all the cool shit that we want to do now that soccer season is over, and I'm excited. Josie told us she made mota cookies in her dorm when she was a freshman, which means she is my ultimate hero. Besides Mila. And Cameron, who I'm secretly in love with. Shhh…don't tell.

14 November 2009

Oh my fucking god. Last night was horribly weird. I ended up going to a party with Mila and Trevor and Calvin. All the sophomore girls on the team came too, and we drank this alcoholic punch stuff with apples in it. Mariah and Bridgette also came; Bridgette doesn't drink but she's still hyper and fun anyway.

I got real drunk and it was fun, but then Calvin and I went to his car to get my purse when I was going to leave, and he proceeded to speed talk lecture me for, like, 20 minutes, accusing me of being the bad guy in our stupid little relationship thing that's been going on. He basically blamed me for everything, like the negative feelings he has felt. When I would try to talk, or defend myself, or explain, he would cut me off and say that I was wrong.

It was probably the most irritating and frustrating thing ever. I remember sitting there and thinking, "Oh my god, I don't even believe this is happening right now!" I was so drunk and he was so pissed and I was thinking that I kind of hate him now. Like, he's seriously the biggest idiot ever!

And he *is* insecure, like all the sophomore girls have told me. I was finally able to get a ride back to the dorms with this random girl that I don't even know. At least it wasn't awkward because I was drunk and didn't give a shit about anything. This morning Calvin called me, probably to apologize, and I didn't answer. Asshole!

15 November 2009

Yesterday I went to Pike Place Market with Kan and her friend Trey from her hometown who is visiting. I wore a cool outfit and wandered around by myself while they were together. It was nice to be there basically alone. It made me feel like a real person and happy.

I got Sawyer presents for his birthday, and I got some poetry zines in this little bookstore. I was reading one and it made me happy because the guy talked about things I worry about, like how we are all alone, and how we are slaves to money and oil. It was reassuring to know someone feels the same and that I'm not crazy.

Last night I slept on the couch in Calvin's apartment and stayed up till, like, 3:30 a.m. talking to Drake and Ed, who is another guy on the soccer team that is really tall and blonde and plays defense. I told all the guys to read the poems from my zine. Then we all started writing our own poems and we put them in a bowl on the counter.

Also, Calvin apologized to me, but I still think he's stupid. It bugs the shit out of me that he never stops talking. Seriously, he can't be quiet for more than two minutes.

Today I wore a gray ruffled dress with a pink sweater, and I got a ton of compliments. Mostly people were like, "Omg, you're wearing pink!" And I was like, "Yeah, it's so weird…" (Sarcasm). But seriously, that's what they said.

I went on a run to Gasworks, and it was sprinkling and a little windy, but not unbearable. When I got to the top of the hill the view of Seattle just made me feel like everything was going to be okay, and that made me feel fucking real. It was beautiful. I swear I could have stood there forever.

The wind was slapping me and everywhere the sky was gray. The grass was twinkling neon green and the gas machines were a brown, coppery, rust-looking color. Vibrant. The water was churning because of the wind. Deep blue, gray-blue. The city lights told me there was something more in the world than being worried about school. The buildings stood as excitement for adventure to come, and I feel like running there every day.

The best part of running is that your body becomes invincible to the weather. It almost allows you to become the rain and the wind since you generate your own heat and can enjoy feeling the cold. If you could be the coldness, that's what it'd be like.

I love looking up at the trees and seeing them bare except for a few yellow leaves at the tips. Sometimes when I run I feel like I'm escaping my body and all the ugly feelings about my weight and worries about caloric intake. I feel like a deer when I run: graceful, lean. I dunno if it looks like that. Maybe I was a deer in another life.

Oh, also, lately I've been wanting to be alone so fucking

badly, and I haven't been able to at all. It sucks. I get irritated with people abnormally quickly, and it sucks when you can't get away. I was in the university library today and I had some alone time while working on my essay. So that was good, even if I was working on homework. I can get it done much faster when I'm not distracted.

I feel like lately people have been misunderstanding me, and it makes me feel uneasy towards myself, like I don't know who I am, which I don't, but sometimes I feel like I do. And if I keep saying that I don't then it will be a self-fulfilling prophecy. I should just start believing that I know who I am.

My interactions with people have been terrible lately, and I think this stems from the fact that I've had too much exposure to people, which isn't the best thing for me. I wanted to say that maybe one of the problems is that I focus too much on myself instead of on others, and that maybe I should stop being selfish and start doing nice things for people I care about.

Maybe this is something I want to change about myself. But I want to do it because I genuinely care about those people, not because I want to feel better about myself, which is what I'm actually feeling, I'm pretty sure.

God, I've been feeling insane lately, like there is too much to think about. So much shit has been running around in my head; it's not very calming. It's actually extremely stressful, but I think writing is making me feel better.

Kan makes me weird sometimes, because I feel like when-ever I tell her something I'm worried about, she shrugs it off like it's not a big deal at all, and it makes me feel like I'm a huge baby or something for getting stressed out about things that don't matter.

Random: I hope these diaries become useful to me, because I was thinking about all the fucking time I have invested in them, and it's kind of insane. Like, this one entry has taken me at least an hour. More, most likely.

It's one in the morning. I need to get out more. Staying on campus with all the creepy Jesus people is not the best thing for me. I need to see the harsh realities of the real universe more often.

20 November 2009

This is the first entry of my new diary. Night before last I slept at Calvin and roommates' apartment, and yesterday I woke up on their couch around seven because they all had to go get their body fat tested and were really loud when they left. Then I woke up again a couple hours later when they got back, when Calvin and Trevor sat on me and rapped about me sleeping. Young money? I dunno.

I went to the student union building yesterday to work on my *Revelations of Divine Love* essay, which by the way is awfully written, but I don't care! I know it's going to be terrible. I can't write ten pages of shit about a god I don't believe in; it just isn't me.

Then Lillian, Kan, and I went to the library and it stressed me out because I felt like Kan and I couldn't talk about serious things with Lillian there. I was stressed out about doing my Logic homework, and I wanted to write my paper, too, but I didn't get to it. I just wanted to be alone, but Lillian follows me around now, kind of. At least when I invite her to something, but I always feel obligated to invite her to where I'm going, even when I don't actually want her to come.

Anyway, later Kan and I ended up getting coffee and going to

Kan's dorm, and then playing Mario at the guys' apartments. I had planned to get all my shit homework done and I didn't. That kind of made me anxious but I realized that I shouldn't worry so much about everything and try to do everything perfectly, because life isn't perfect.

Everything's going to be all right, because I'm a real person and I can learn things and fail at things. I can have weaknesses and be less than superior at certain activities. So I'll get it done when I get it done. And if I don't, fuck it!

Today I woke up and I felt really good, like everything is okay and is going to work out. I felt real. And happy. It was strange! Because I never feel real or happy. So far my day has been good. I got coffee before my Japanese class, and we watched Godzilla movies all class period.

This kid Ezra talked to me in that class, and I feel like he is real and likes cool things and is someone I could actually say real things to. He asked for my phone number so I think we are friends. He has super blonde hair and blonde, bushy eyebrows and is sort of cute but not really. His sister is a year older and lives on my floor in the dorms.

I'm going to take Psychology next quarter because Kan, Lia, and Lillian are taking it, and I'm going to have to take it eventually to fulfill some exploratory credit. I want to take Imaginative Writing but I'm not eligible because my writing scores from high school haven't been generated yet. I might have to take another class before it. Lately I've been feeling like my head is going to explode, and I've been trying to feel clear-headed.

I want to be like my brother. I want to *be* the view from Gasworks. I want to be a part of something meaningful, like a secret political revolution. Anarchy or nihilism. I want to not worry about anything. I don't want to be afraid of talking to people. I want to find someone interesting and ask him a billion questions. And I want people to come up to me and be interested in who I am and ask me a billion questions. Like Kan did when we first became good friends.

I'm glad I'm using this notebook as my diary because I just had it in my drawer being useless. Now it has a purpose. I've been wanting to shed things off that I don't use, or use things all up so I can get rid of them. Simplification sounds sexy to me.

I'm excited for the future, and I hate those moments where I don't feel that way. Ana, please remember that nothing matters, and please have fun and be okay. Don't take everything so seriously! The consequences usually don't add up to death. And if they did, then so be it. Death is a relief from life.

21 November 2009

Today I woke up at 6:16 a.m. to go work at this clementine stand at a sports complex with Kan and Calvin, and it wasn't too bad. We handed out little clementines and other free stuff to the public, and played soccer. We watched soccer, too, because there was a tournament there. It was actually fun, kinda. And we get paid for it, so that's cool.

Sometimes watching soccer puts me in a bad mood because it reminds me of my college experience with soccer and how shitty that was and is. So for a while I was pissed because of that, and also because Kan makes me feel like shit sometimes. She is *extremely* critical of everyone, but then when it comes to herself she makes excuses about why she did something bad. And it's usually not her fault, or else she did it because of someone else telling her to, like an authority figure.

Ugh, it's frustrating! She criticizes me a lot, or just says mean things. I'm a sensitive person and I'm already way hard on myself anyway, so it adds fuel to the fire.

22 November 2009

Today we worked again at the clementine booth, but only until one in the afternoon, which was nice. We didn't have to stand out in the rain and wind under that huge ridiculous tent, either. We got to stay under the overhang of the building.

I drove Kan and I there with Mila's car. I felt in control of myself and less lost. Lost mentally. Kan's been mean lately, and I don't think she knows who I am. She acts like she does, though, and like I'm inferior. She just says rude stuff randomly, or whenever I say something she'll negate me and act like it was stupid of me to mention it.

A lot of the time I say things and I don't know why I say them, or ask questions that have obvious answers, and these are the moments that she replies with something rude. I think I say these things to fill up space, because I find that I know the answer right after I ask the question. Ugh, I hate this.

Today when we were working I was making a sign that said "free take one" in cursive and when Kan saw it she said, "Don't write it in cursive, no one will be able to read it!" But she said it so that it sounded like I was an idiot for doing that. I was thinking, *Okay, well why the fuck would you say that? Because it's fucking fine, it doesn't even matter!*

She says unnecessary rude things like this, and it hurts my feelings. A lot of the time it's her tone, not specifically what

48

she says, but it still hurts me. Maybe I'm sensitive, but still, what's the point of saying shit like that? I don't know, this is really bothering me.

This always happens to me! Every time I become close to someone and/or vulnerable with them, I always get it turned around on me and they act superior. I'm not saying that I am superior to begin with or anything; the relationship should be equal. But it's like they become super controlling and I hate being micromanaged or controlled with regard to pointless shit.

This is why I hate people! Because they are assholes. And the worst thing is that I do stuff like this, too, only because I'm human. I don't realize this, when I do it, I mean. I dunno if Kan does either. It's in her nature I think, the whole critical thing.*

I feel like I'm pretty good at being reasonable with people and calming them down, and making them let me do my own thing. I hate when people try to control me or act superior to me because it's not a competition. Or at least I don't want it to be because it makes me so tired. I feel like Kan does this a lot. Makes it into a competition, I mean. Maybe I've just had too much of her lately. I don't know. I don't want to think about this anymore.

[*Ana: Kan has Mars in Gemini and a Virgo Moon... –J.]

26 November 2009

Home! Today is Thanksgiving. It was delicious, we already ate. I'm very proud of myself because I didn't stuff myself. I've had, like, three or four glasses of wine and I'm feeling good.

Yesterday I flew home at 6:40 a.m. Calvin drove me to the airport. I slept over at his apartment on the top bunk of his bed and we got up at 3:56 a.m. We talked till at least midnight, so I barely got any sleep. I read *Self* on the plane, a book by Yann Martel that I bought recently. It is beautiful and fucked up. He is a spectacular writer. I think that if I could be anyone other than myself (and Björk and Angelina Jolie) I'd be Yann Martel.

But anyway, I only got, like, three or four hours of sleep, and I never took a nap because Grandma, my aunt, and Camila came over from Lewiston and surprised me! We went shopping at the mall and Grandma bought us all boots, it was kickass badass. I got zombie-killing ones, at least they look like they would be good at stomping on zombies' faces.

I slept in my own bed, too. It was strange waking up and seeing everything I saw and lived in during high school and not Natalie and Lillian. I like waking up alone; it makes me feel like myself. It's been lovely being home, although being here too long would get irritating.

Sawyer and Lacy are here. Sawyer quit his job in LA and I think he's going to get a job as a ski instructor in McCall. Which would be cool, I guess, but I want him to move to Seattle and get an apartment so I could hang out over there all the time. I think that would be liberating. Like, I would have a life, haha.

I imagine myself taking the bus there and back. For some reason I feel real when I leave campus and do something exciting, because when I come back I feel like I have things other than school.

Oh my god, I forgot to tell you that Kan and I got drunk together for the first time! We got Molly, who is 21, to buy us sparkling wine, which we drank in the cafeteria and the library. We each had our own bottle and drank the whole thing. And *nothing* happened. So we got Becky, who is also 21, to buy us real wine, and we went to the empty apartment at the guys' complex and got super shwasted. It was so much fun.

Ed, Drake, Trevor, Calvin, and Ronan saw us when we tried to sneakily go pee in their bathroom, and they took pictures of us laughing and rolling around on the floor. It was funny. We secretly liked the attention. We wrote poems, too, and the next day when we were sober and hung-over they were fucking hilarious! It was great, I'm proud of us.

Today Camila and I went to a coffee shop and worked on homework, and got some coffee and got high on caffeine. I edited my essay on *Godzilla*, and I am proud of it because my teacher said it is articulate and that there is a certain beauty to my writing, and that made me feel really good about myself. You don't even know.

And now I feel happy. I don't want that to be only because I'm kinda tipsy. I want it to be real. I feel like everything's going to be okay. Now I'm going to go help Mom with the pie she's making. Love you.

29 November 2009

I don't feel well. Mentally. Actually, I feel like loads of shit. Yesterday we went to a huge bookstore and despair sunk into my skin like fast-acting LSD. I went to the Buddhism section, like always, and it fucked with my mind. I feel like every-thing I do is wrong or bad, and that I'm not diligent or able to work hard, and I feel materialistic because we were shopping all day and buying things and it made us happy.

I don't want to have all these attachments and I can't love anyone! I don't know what love is because how can it possibly exist when humans only have their own individual desires in mind? I'm just confused, and I feel like my whole life is fucked and I'm worth nothing and I've been doing it wrong this whole time.

I was reading about illusions and reality, and, I dunno, it was just so bad. I dunno what anything is, like consciousness and awareness and who I am, and I've been freaking out inside, and I cried last night and, like, thrice today.

The day before yesterday we went shopping, and I stole a *ton* of shit. Here's the list: hair dye, five chapsticks, shoes, a ring, earrings, a bracelet, and I think that might be all. But, oh my god. I started to look for something to take in every store, and that made me feel materialistic also, and weird because I was thinking, well, I don't have to pay for anything so why would I *ever* buy anything?

Then, my homework's been stressing me out very badly, and it really is not a big deal. I have to do a five-minute presentation for my Japanese class and that is freaking me out because talking in front of a group of people is my biggest fear. I don't want school to be my life. I want to have a life and have school be only a small part of it.

I'm never going to escape the cycle of life and death, or achieve Nirvana, because I have school, and I don't have time to actually practice Buddhism, and I don't know if it's even true, but I feel like it is. Then I feel like I'm not trying hard enough, and I also feel like I'm only going through the motions of what a person is supposed to do, and not living how I want to live. And I've just been feeling so down.

Today was also the worst ever. I flew back to Seattle early

and took the bus back to school, but it took forever because I did half of it wrong and got lost in Seattle. I was walking the streets for so long with my fucking huge suitcase and hating my life and wondering what the fucking purpose of all this shit is, and wanting to not exist ever again.

After I *finally* found the correct bus stop after wandering for a long time I sat there for 15 minutes in the cold. When I got to school I went to the guys' apartments to get my Logic book, and Calvin unlocked the door for me and didn't even say a word to me. He went back to bed without even saying hi. I was crying because everything was shit, and he didn't even notice; he just walked back to his room. He isn't a real person, he doesn't understand anything.

I walked back to my dorm up the huge fucking hill with my massive heavy suitcase. It sucked. When I finally got back to my room I went straight to sleep and slept for a few hours. It was a relief. Then Lillian came back and I had to talk to her when human contact was the last thing I desired. But I got all my crap unpacked and organized, which was good.

I don't want to do anything anymore. I get upset when I realize that there are people that love me and care about me. It's hard for me to love myself. I need something and I don't know what it is.*

Calvin just called me and we talked for 40 seconds and he asked me what was wrong and I said nothing, and he said, "That's a lie," and I said "Okay." He is so stupid.

[*Ana: IT'S ASTROLOGY!!! ASTROLOGY IS WHAT YOU NEED!!! –J.]

30 November 2009

Today was…good. I think. I found out in my Japanese class today that I don't have to present until Friday! And we watched this Japanese show called *Nobuta Wo Produce*, which was about high school, and the main character thought exactly how I feel! It was comforting.

In Logic we had an exam and I finished before everyone. I thought it was super easy so hopefully I'll get a good grade.

Then in my Middle Ages class Sam told me he likes me. In a strange note-writing session we had. He was basically like, "I love you." And I was like, "No, you don't, you're a freak." I think he does like me though, which is cool, I guess. He's pretty cute. But I still don't trust him because he obviously cannot love me; he doesn't even know me.

Oh, and also, I got a B on our ten page paper! The *Revelations of Divine Love* one. I was excited about that because I totally bullshitted the entire thing.

I ran around Gasworks as well and it felt good because I haven't run in a long while.

Another thing that was awesome about today is that my roommates have been gone all day because of this huge choir concert that they are both in. It's 9:34 p.m. and they're still not back! So I got to be by myself. I listened to a lot of music and worked on my Hello Kitty paper, which is what my five-minute presentation is about. Tomorrow I don't have class so I'll hopefully get a lot done.

Calvin texted me today, too, and said that he misses me, and I was like, "haha okay." I am going to try to not go over there for a long time because I don't want to be around him because he isn't a real person.

I really tried to not be stressed today, and it worked. I am going to try to read more, and do stuff that isn't my home-work, like crochet and watch movies and drink wine and run and write. I am going to realize that I will get through it and everything will be okay.

02 December 2009

Today was weird. Classes were blah. Except for Middle Ages; that was when I began feeling super stressed and anxious. For no reason. It sucked. It was too cold in the room and I felt gross and fat and ugly.

Kan's been rude lately…big surprise. She's just great at putting you down, you know? Like, she told me I looked like a boy with my haircut (I got a haircut when I was home) and I was like, "Oh, thank you!" But seriously, why would she say that? No idea, and she brought it up more than once. I don't get why she has to put me down all the time, and criticize. It's fucking irritating.

Anyway, I'm trying not to dwell on this. I'm trying to have good replies, like not necessarily mean ones, but ones that get the point across that she's being a bitch, or that what she's saying is rude and irrelevant and pointless, or that I don't give a fuck about her opinion. That being said, I'm going to forget about it and quit giving her opportunities to put me down. I'm not going to complain about or criticize myself or my features.

Today I went running by Gasworks, and I was listening to the "Hello Seattle" remix by Owl City, and right when I got to the top of the hill the song got to the intense part. It was like I was in a movie; it was perfect. The sky was cloudless and illuminated by a pink and orange glow from the sun dripping down the sides of the skyscrapers. I knew that there was something incredibly important about that moment.

What I felt was that people are terrible to each other, and for no reason. It's beautiful when people love each other and are kind and open-minded; that's what the world needs in order to function. I don't understand why people are always competing against each other, or comparing to see who's better. It doesn't make any sense.

We need to give each other the benefit of the doubt, not judge or criticize, because you can never completely understand a person or her situation unless you are her. It felt like enlightenment up there. I realized that all I need is confidence and assurance and everything will be okay. Because in reality things are okay and will work out. They always do, it's just my feelings that ruin everything. My anxiety.

Something else that happened today was that I went to a free concert on campus with Kan and some other people that are in her music class, like a couple of the soccer girls and Charles, a guy on the men's soccer team that Cameron says looks like he runs like a person that used to be obese but is now skinny. Which is hilarious because I never would have thought of something like that, but after she said it I was like holy shit, he actually does run like that.

I sat next to him at the concert and he's super nice. Like when you talk to him he asks you questions like he really cares, and it felt so good. Calvin and Sam never ask me about things that matter, or about anything interesting at all. They are terrible conversationalists. It's dumb and it makes me feel alone inside my own head.

Anyway, the last few songs were jazzy and it was alluring. There was a flute player who was extremely talented, and a guy on the bongos who *was* the rhythms he beget. I envisioned the music flowing from their instruments. I know that what they were attempting to create is something sublime, something bigger than being human, and they succeeded. I was so moved when I experienced that. Not only when I heard that music, but when I felt how important that was, and how I was lucky enough to experience it.

I just realized both my good experiences today involved music, and that shows how influential it can be. It can make you feel things you would never have felt without it, or feel things more intensely. It's like a drug almost. I feel kind of disappointed that I'm not able to feel these things without it. Or feel the sublime powers of the universe, or realize that there's something bigger than me, or be humbled by the water and the sky and the buildings, or realize that life is all right and change happens and time goes on, and everything will be okay.

Without music I dunno what I'd do, because feeling all those things is essential to my being. It keeps me alive when I'm stumbling around, blinded by apathy and knowing that I'm worthless. Knowing, not just feeling.

04 December 2009

I presented my Hello Kitty project in my Japanese class and I'm glad it's over.

Yesterday was weird, regarding my mentality. Natalie, Lillian, and I got dressed up and went downtown to the Seattle Art Museum because it's free the first Thursday of every month. It was weird because I loved it; the art and the people there were interesting. But then I started to feel bad. I felt like I am not as interesting as those people, or able to talk intelligently about anything, because they all looked really knowledgeable. I was confused about the art because some of it looked like I could have done it, and I don't understand how certain artists get to be famous.

I felt lost and hopeless and like no one loved or cared about me. All irrational feelings. I want to be an artist but I can't draw, and how else can I express my feelings? My words are awful, my vocabulary pitiful, my poetry horrendous. I can't express myself. I want to be able to draw, but I can't.

How can I establish myself as important or influential in any way? I don't know. This seems important. What am I going to do with my fucking boring life?

08 December 2009

Yesterday I had my Logic final and it went well, I think. I got a 100% on our last test and I have a 95% in the class, so I'm not particularly worried.

I went to Ezra's dorm last night to study for our Japanese final today. He is pretty cool, I guess. The reason we hung out is because the other day Kan and I drank the rest of our wine we've been saving, and it wasn't enough to get drunk off of, but enough to be like, "Whoa, definite change!" I texted Ezra, "omg drunk," and that started things. I feel like I made a new friend, so it's cool.

09 December 2009

At dinner today I made a friend…or she made a friend, because I definitely do not count her as my friend. Her name is Audrey and she's a sophomore. She started talking to me while I was reading in the cafeteria. We started talking about religion and I told her about my ongoing interest in Buddhism. And she basically told me that Buddhism is bad and I should believe in Christianity and go to church.

It sucks being preached to. I hate arguing with people; it's pointless, especially when I know they are wrong and they are so sure they are right. So I just nodded a lot and was like, "yeah." But it put me in a bad mood because of her close-mindedness and utter belief in a system without questioning it. Especially because she was raised as a Christian and has been going to a specific church since she was five.

She's brainwashed and it's crazy how people think they are right when they are taught to believe something and never once question it's validity.* They never ask why! Think for yourself you fucking asshole! But whatever, I don't want to think about this anymore.

[*Ana: It's the exact same concept regarding eating animals and their secretions and using animals as products. It's crazy how passionately people will defend their right to pay other people to kill animals so that they can feast on their flesh and wear their skin, only because they were raised to think of such things as normal and acceptable. Then they say they love animals, when they really only love being the owner of animals, to exploit them at will.

We live in a world full of ignorant psychopaths, always ready to pillage and plunder, abuse and misuse, and profit from others' suffering. Better get used to it, you're gonna be here for a while. All you can do is avoid those people; they'll never disappear completely.

Compassion is the logic of the wise. Flee from those who find this difficult to understand. –J.]

10 December 2009

Yesterday Ezra came over to my dorm and we played backgammon and he has a fucking attention disorder or something and could barely play. He kept knocking over all the pieces and rambling on and on about random stuff. He is ridiculous! I'm pretty sure he's in love with me because when I had to walk to Kan's dorm to help her pack he walked me halfway because his dorm is halfway there. He ended up never helping his sister pack, which is why he came up to my dorm in the first place.

Kan and I moved all our shit into the empty apartment at the soccer guys' complex, which is where we are going to secretly stay for five days when the dorms close for Christmas break. We are also going to a concert during break before we go home. Muse, Phoenix, Vampire Weekend, Metric. Holy fuck. It's going to be mind-blowing. I love all those bands!

Anyway, today was blah. I texted Ezra a lot. But he's weird. He never asks me anything about myself and that bothers me. I'm starting to think he's not real, like all the other boys that are interested in me.

11 December 2009

I feel like I could easily go insane in the room Kan and I are staying in. Bare walls and only one window. And silence. Maybe I feel that way because everyone is gone. Also, I feel kind of scared and paranoid because the room/apartment building/hallway reminds me of the place the girl in my book got raped in. It was gross and degrading and frightening and vulgar, and maybe that's why I feel nervous there.

I'm kind of scared to go outside when it's dark, and now it gets dark at, like, 5:30 p.m., so I can never do anything! I think Kan and I are going to run at eight tonight, and it'll be okay because we'll be together. I'm feeling weird, kinda anxious.

Something I've realized: you should try new things because if you hate it you can always go back to doing what you did before, or try something else. When you do something new you should always give it time because you need to get accustomed to it in order to actually enjoy it.

In the beginning, things are bad or uncomfortable at times, but it gets better! If you want to do something, then do it! Don't make excuses like you didn't want it anyway. Don't be afraid that you'll make mistakes or that you will fail.

I want to experience new things! I want to travel! I want to get accustomed to change!

13 December 2009

We went to the movies today. *The Men Who Stare at Goats*. I thought it was hilarious and Kan thought it was stupid.

14 December 2009

Today we rode the bus downtown and went to the Seattle public library, which is breathtaking! There are at least ten stories, and a million people, and the walls are geometric and made of windows. We got library cards and spent a couple hours exploring. We walked to Pike Place Market afterwards and explored there as well.

Tomorrow is the Muse concert! I'm excited to see them, and also to go home and see my family.

HOLY SHIT. MIND BLOWN. The concert is over and it was spectacular. I wish I could find good enough words to describe it, but I'm not the best poet for the job. In essence, it was beautiful, especially considering how intensely people can feel when they hear music and how much emotion was brought forward.

Musicians hold a distinct power, and I admire how much effort they put into their art. On stage they're completely themselves, absolutely genuine. Especially the mature bands like Muse. They know exactly what they're doing and they are confident and unafraid and I adore that.

When they played "Knights of Cydonia" I felt powerful and free and courageous and that I'm human and it's meaningful for me to feel things. I could feel energy flowing outwards from me and I jumped and danced and lost myself in those vibrations. Best vibes ever.

Metric was fantastic, too! The lead singer wore a sweet outfit and the energy she brought onstage was lovely. I look up to her, I think she's fabulous! Phoenix was kickass also. They were cute too, ha. Vampire Weekend was cool, and 30 Seconds to Mars just seemed stupid to me, like immature and for high-schoolers. I didn't like that band that much to begin with, but now I really don't like them.

I don't want to sound pretentious or anything, the lead singer just seemed too into himself, and he said 'fuck' a lot, and not poetically. Swear words can be used as poetry, but he made it seem like he thought he was a badass when he swore, and I thought it was something an annoying and rude 16-year-old would do. Like all the people I hated when I was in high school.

Anyway, in the very beginning Kan and I fought our way to the front, which I'm still considering a major feat. I don't know how we stayed up there, but we did throughout the whole show, which was like five or six hours. We were right behind the first line of people, it was cool.

But, oh my god, it was so hot and claustrophobic in there, it was ridiculous. Everyone was thirsty. Drake and his brother and Ed came also; we carpooled. We ran to the show from the car because we were kind of late and it was far away. It was fun running in the dark and being all excited. It felt like James Bond. I saw Ezra there for, like, three minutes after it was over, we had been texting a lot today talking about nothing.

Kan left for home tonight at the same time as Ed and Calvin, so I'm alone in our room. All her stuff is gone. It's nice being alone, though. I needed a break from her. Tomorrow Drake and his brother are going to drive me to the airport. I get to go home!

Oh, also, Calvin and I kissed today, just for fun. Even though we are not supposed to anymore, since we basically ended things between us. Oh, well. I like kissing.

20 December 2009

Today I finished reading *The Alchemist*, and I started reading *The Wisdom of Insecurity* which is very good, enlightening. Been home for a few days now.

On Thursday I had an appointment with my gynecologist, and I talked to him about my anxiety and depression, and he gave me a prescription for Zoloft*. So I'm taking pills now. I dunno what to say, how I feel. I almost cried a little talking to him about it, and I felt really stupid because I feel like there's no reason for me to ever feel bad.

I'm still trying to deal with my existence. It's frustrating. I'm scared. And worried. I had a panic attack after I took the first pill. I cried because it felt like there was an airplane flying through my mind carrying my thoughts, and it was like there was fear attached to each thought, like those planes that have messages on banners attached to them.

Mom freaked out because I was so scared. I feel like she just made it worse because she looked at me like I was a crazy person while I tried to explain to her about the airplanes, and it didn't feel good. It's been better, though. My feelings of worry and fear are only fleeting, ephemeral now.

I still don't know if I'm making this up in my head, if I even need pills, or if I'm over-exaggerating. I feel weak, idiotic. Down, kinda. Tired. It's sometimes hard to concentrate. I was afraid to write. I thought it'd confuse me, my perception of who I am. Don't want to go in depth.

[*Ana: This will fuck up your sex drive and is only masking your symptoms without directly addressing their root cause. Trying consistent meditation first is advised. –J.]

27 December 2009

Christmas was brilliant! I got everything I asked for, which was, like, three things. And everyone liked what I got them. Sawyer really liked the book to hide things in, and his cardboard speakers from Urban Outfitters, and his Ol' Dirty Bastard shirt. I was glad.

We went to see *Zombieland* at the dollar theatre so I could wear my zombie-killing boots and all my new stuff. It was a pretty cool movie, except the main character was all awkward and reminded me of Davis and I don't like thinking about Davis.

Yesterday we went skiing and Sawyer didn't have to work the whole time (he's a ski instructor) so we got to ski with him. We played tag a lot, which we always did when we were little. We visited the cabin he's staying at for a little while, and I ate a shit-load of his peanut M&M's and looked at his books on the coffee table. He has *Naked Lunch*, which is one I want to read. Right now I'm reading *The Book Thief* because I got it for Christmas.

I finished this book about Buddhism called *Hardcore Zen* on Christmas Eve night. It made a lot of sense and kind of straightened my mind out, which is good for me. Thanks Brad Warner! I'm going to buy the other book he wrote because I got a gift card to a bookstore.

Sawyer got me moccasins, which is the third thing I asked for, and I got my Hello Kitty toaster and a fisheye camera, which were the other things I asked for. I've been taking cool pics! I can do multiple and long exposures, it's sweet. I'm excited to see how they come out.

05 January 2010

Back in Seattle already. Yesterday Drake and Kan picked me up from the airport, and everything was fine. We had a soccer meeting and it was fun seeing everyone. It made me happy because I can have a fresh start with soccer and figure out my mind.

Tomorrow is the first day of classes! I have Psychology, Ethics, and Foundations, which is a required class and I think it has something to do with religion.

Kan and I watched *I Heart Huckabees*. It was brilliant and had Buddhist connotations, and it made so much sense to me. We also made ramen in her dorm and talked about our minds and had deep conversations and it was nice. I was reaffirmed of her being my best friend here.

Right now I'm in the cafeteria. I've had my first two classes. I'm going to have a lot of work ahead of me, but it's okay. I think Psych will be interesting, and it'll be nice because Kan, Lia, and Lillian are in that class as well, so I'll easily be able to stay on top of everything.

Foundations is entirely about Christianity, which makes me uneasy, but I think I should be positive about it because the more I understand it, the more I can be reaffirmed of my Buddhist nature. Haha. I think the less ignorant I am in the subject is better, and I'll be able to figure myself out more. No fear. I am not afraid to be immersed in something I don't believe in. I am accepting, I will embrace it. But that doesn't mean that it has to define me.

07 January 2010

There are things to be said. Ethics was only, like, 30 minutes long because our professor had to go do something important, which was whatever. It was interesting from what I heard in that short period of time. Also, our professor is fucking sexy and if he wasn't happily married I would seriously get on that shit. Haha, just kidding. He's in his 50's I think. But he really is beautiful. He wears great outfits. I think he's been through a lot of stuff, and he seemed wise, so I respect him.

This morning at 9:30 we had the weight room walk-through

and it was okay, I guess. I dunno why, but it makes me super fucking self-conscious and nervous to be in a weight room and be working out. Why do I always feel like I'm doing it wrong or that I look stupid? I dunno, but I hate it. It's all in my head.

I need to be more confident, and I know this! Kan's being critical doesn't help either. But, you know what? I'm going to lose the pride and use this as an obstacle that will make me gain more confidence. I'm going to forget everything. I'm going to forget it because it doesn't fucking matter.

I'm real and I'm going to do my best and be myself and not think about what other people are thinking. I am not going to worry! *Fuck* my mind, I'm throwing you out because you're such a backstabber and a betrayer. I love myself and I'm safe. I'm not going to worry about being good enough. I can do it, I've always done it. I'm not self-conscious. I don't give a fuck about anything.

In this moment, right here, I am safe. I am all right. Here is what exists now: the embrace of tan caffeine. Silence in the cafeteria. The pen and paper in my lap. And that's it, nothing else. No worries, no anxieties. School is interesting and I'm going to learn things I want to know more about.

I'm not going to run tonight because I don't want to. People are nice. I'm healthy. I'm strong. I've dealt with my existence this far and I haven't given up. I have a fresh start every morning when I wake up. I believe in myself. I'm going to wear a crazy outfit tomorrow and I'm going to be who I am.

09 January 2010

All right, fuck my life. I keep trying to be alone and people keep attacking me! At the cafeteria yesterday I was sitting right by the door because I'm dumb, and Jean and Zara came in and saw me and decided to sit with me. Which is fine because I like them, but I just really, really wanted to be alone and write. Oh, well.

Zara is this tiny black girl from Oregon and is super nice, and Jean is from Washington and is pretty overweight, with curly dark hair. She hangs out with Natalie and Lillian in my room sometimes. Both Zara and Jean live on my floor in the dorms. They are only acquaintances, I guess. Then Drake came and talked to us, and I felt less awkward because I feel more comfortable around him since I've known him longer.

Then I went to Ethics and it was so interesting! I love my professor. He told the class that he takes Zoloft for anxiety! We're twins! It made me feel real and like things were all right.

I went to dinner with Ezra and his friends because Kan went home for a couple days. I like hanging out with guys. Ezra's roommate calls me "anime girl" since I'm the girl from Ezra's Japanese class.

After dinner Ezra and I watched *Howl's Moving Castle* on my computer. And this is where the worst thing in the entire world occurred. I fucking LEAKED my PERIOD on his FUCKING bed sheets. NOT KIDDING. WORST DAY OF MY LIFE!!! Holy fuck it was extremely embarrassing!

It sucked because I could feel it happening, but I couldn't get up and check because for a long while his friends were in the room hanging out and talking to us after the movie ended. I couldn't be like, "Um, can you guys leave so I can check that my period isn't leaking?" If I got up to check and it wasn't leaking, I could play it off and act like I was getting into a more comfortable position, but if it was leaking then everyone would see it, so I couldn't move.

Also, sometimes it feels like it's leaking, but it actually isn't, so I was just hoping that it wasn't. But I was fucking WRONG!! I feel like if it had only been Ezra, I could have discreetly checked somehow. In the end, when I finally got up, I saw it and was like fuuuuuuuuuck. I had to tell him, there was no way I could get around it.

I felt too awkward and it was just awful! But he acted very understanding and said it was okay and that he has sisters and isn't too immature to deal with stuff like that, which was reassuring, I guess, but I was still mortified.

I was thinking, the whole situation could have been much worse, like his friends could have been in there when I was forced to tell him. I'm glad that didn't happen. I left as fast as I could, and when I got back to my dorm my roommates were gone, best thing *ever.* So I had a little freak out session alone in my room.

I felt like hiding in a 30-foot-deep, black pit. Ugh. I still feel that way. Oh, but Zara stopped by my room after that happened and we talked and watched TV, and it was nice because she has a really calm demeanor and I didn't feel awkward.

Anyway, that was how yesterday went for me. Now I'm in the coffee shop on campus. I want to be by myself. I guess I've been feeling a bit anxious. Zoloft's definitely been helping, though. It kind of lets me step back and view the situation without being absorbed by it. It's weird. It seems like it helps me be more rational and objective about my feelings.

Apparently I am going shopping with River today, my super tall and fashionable friend from high school, because he's coming to Seattle. He might sleep in the empty apartment at the guys' complex, but I'm not sure.

10 January 2010

Yesterday was interesting. River and I went to H&M and American Apparel and a bookstore. We took night pics with my fisheye at Pike's. We decided to sleep in the empty apartment at the guys' complex, only to be caught by campus security, also known as the fake police, and it was so stupid.

I'm supposed to email my dorm's manager about it. I think maybe he manages all the apartment buildings and dorms on campus, which is probably why I have to talk to him. I dunno what's going to happen, probably nothing too extreme. Maybe a fine. River is banned from campus. I had to ride in the police car back to my dorm after they questioned us. Ughhh.

11 January 2010

I dyed my hair blue. People keep saying it looks like cotton candy. I re-did the pink I had before and also re-bleached my roots. Tabby, the girl I sat next to in my Middle Ages class, let me use her dye. She lives in my dorm on a different floor.

I like Tabby because she is happy and talkative and likes to do "bad" things like drink and hook up with guys. She is also extremely overweight, and is always hooking up exclusively with black guys, which is funny to me because it's such a stereotype. A lot of black guys seem to like obese, white women. I don't know why! Not that it even matters, it's just so random to me. And seeing a common stereotype be reaffirmed in such a strong manner, when often I doubt that stereotypes are even true, is kind of fascinating.

13 January 2010

Tomorrow's my birthday! Kan and I went downtown yester-day, and I got my lip pierced! It looks kickass badass, I'm super happy and excited.

14 January 2010

Today we had to get up at six and do sprints for soccer. Winter workouts are sprints in the gym.

At the end I thought I was going to throw up, so I laid on the ground, and Cameron came over and told me to sit up and helped me up, and I think I'm in love with her. It's the weirdest, most confusing thing ever, but I seriously want her. It's because she is good at everything and extremely intelligent, but still is reckless with intoxicants and that inspires me.

I had a meeting with my dorm's manager about the whole apartment thing with River, and it's going to be okay. I'm thinking I'm going to have to do community service. I secretly like being a delinquent. I have to do community service for my psych class anyway, so it doesn't matter. I have to talk about it with Chadwick, though, which is the only thing that makes me nervous. I don't understand why I have to tell him.

Kan and I went to a coffee shop and she bought me a coffee for my birthday, and gave me a card she made for me. I do think she is my best friend, even though it feels like I talk negatively about her in here. I also got a package from Mom and it had a ton of stuff in it!

Lots of people told me happy birthday. Molly brought cookies to practice, which I ate even though I felt like puking at the time, and they were delicious. Oh, and everyone has liked my lip ring so far, I feel badass!

18 January 2010

This weekend I went to Kan's house! We went shopping in Portland and I decided that I belong there. Because all the people are interesting and grunge and nice. Nicer than the people in Seattle, at least. I met her whole family and they had made cupcakes for my birthday and let me blow out candles. Everything they did was so nice and I felt loved, which was the best feeling.

21 January 2010

Kan isn't here right now, but other than that I have been with her constantly. It's strange that I have a best friend and I can talk to her. My whole life I've been avoiding people and thinking that being alone is better, but I dunno. My views are changing and I think it's good. Basically I'm wondering if it's the Zoloft. It's making things much better.

I just don't know if I'm supposed to feel good, or if it is bad that I'm often in a good mood. Because I feel like I'm not supposed to always feel good, but I guess I don't really. It's weird. I feel like being happy or in a good mood isn't me. Like, it's not in my personality, but the Zoloft is making it a part of my personality. I dunno.

Life is fucking strange. It's not easy having a thinking, opinionated mind. With feelings. It's fucking weird.

24 January 2010

This weekend has been great. Both Friday and Saturday

nights we got real drunk. Kan was there and it was awesome. She hooked up with Adin! It was funny because he's, like, 25, but also a senior on the guys' soccer team, because he was a foreign exchange student and then decided to stay here. And he's so gross.

Friday night I smoked four cigarettes and met a ton of people. I smoked hookah for the first time as well. It was gross. It kind of gave me a headache. I made out with this drug dealer named John who had a lip ring, too. His is on the same side as mine so that when we kissed they were on opposite sides. Haha.

Kan and I walked John to his apartment across from the soccer guys' apartments after the party was over. He was staying with a friend, I think. I forced Kan to come back to my dorm instead of staying at Adin's, and I basically got us all home. I'm actually proud of myself for being responsible even though I was drunk.

Then on Saturday we had the party at the Jungle, the senior girls' house. It was cool because I wore my white minidress with the huge ruffled shoulders and everyone liked it.

Cameron kept giving Kan and I shots, and I smoked a lot of mota with Cameron. The cops came at the very end and asked us if the party was starting or ending, and Kan and I were like, "It's ending!" Then later that night we went to Adin's and people kept saying, "I heard you talked to the cops!" It was hilarious because they thought we were badass. Which we are, I guess.

Lillian and Zara came too, I dunno if they drank, though. I don't think Lillian did. I kept going up to them and being like, "OMG are you having fun?!" Ezra's sister was there and I drunkenly told her I was in love with him (why did I do that??) and she said he has a girlfriend! What the fuck?! Haha, oh well, he is dumb. I don't think he is even that attractive, to be honest. I think if I were super drunk I would probably want to hook up with him. Being sober, probably not.

On Friday we had practice. We actually played soccer instead of only running in the morning. It was fun. I have confidence. I'm feeling much better about myself, it's liberating. And weird. Life may be bearable.

26 January 2010

Today we had a workout at 9:15 a.m. and it was hard. But I'm not dead. I feel like it's never as bad as I imagine it's going to be. I'm feeling good mentally. I can feel my confidence, it's strange. I'm also not afraid of things anymore. Like, I find myself feeling less awkward around people and not afraid to talk to them.

I have very hairy legs.

I'm a fucking badass.

28 January 2010

Today was a good day! Mom sent me a package with Nutella. And I told Kan that I'm taking Zoloft, and we talked about stuff.

I covered a box I have with magazine clippings and put all my books in it. I finished *The Book Thief* and I'm gonna read *Siddhartha* now because it's short.

I got a 93% on my Psych test!

The workout this morning was easy because it was only stations, and each station was only, like, a minute or so long.

02 February 2010

Yesterday was Kan's birthday!

I want to go downtown all the time and do homework or just relax. I want to find a Buddhist place. I want to live a real life. And be unafraid to follow a path, create a path.

I finished reading *Siddhartha*. I need to figure things out. I need to find a Buddhist place, I think it's essential. Maybe I'll do it tomorrow and look up when to go tonight. This is going to happen. This is me finding myself. I need to figure myself out the hard way. I need to fuck things up. I need my mistakes.

04 February 2010

All right. Yesterday I rode the bus downtown to try and find the Buddhist place I found online, and I failed. I could not find the stop I was supposed to get off at, so after I had gone really far I just got off and rode the bus back. I was scared because all the people on the bus looked creepy and we kept getting farther and farther away from downtown, and we were, like, in the middle of nowhere.

And I dunno. I feel like that was real life and I can't do real life because I suck. I'm very sheltered here. What would I do, how would I react, if something crazy actually happened to me? Would I be terrified? I don't want to be. When I get scared like that I feel like I'm going to freeze up and not be able to think rationally, and that scares me even more. It's fucking weird how nervous I get.

05 February 2010

Today in Foundations we had a class discussion and while we did that I wrote stuff down that has been confusing me lately on a piece of paper, and I think I figured stuff out. It felt good.

The new recruits come today and we are meeting them in Chadwick's office at 2:55. We also have team play at 3:30. I dunno how that's going to go. I feel weird right now. Like jittery.

Here is what I wrote in class:

• Seeking wisdom and truth. Finding wisdom?

• Christianity is lovely; people are searching for goodness and love. This is good, great! Life is a cycle, a circle. Evil leaves only to return.

• "Be ye a lamp unto yourself." –Buddha

• I am looking for knowledge and truth and philosophy and words and thoughts, who I am, and love.

• I'm going to seek guidance, but form my own opinions and be an individual. I'm going my own way, but I need help because I'm human.

• I don't believe in heaven or hell. It isn't relevant because what exists now is the world now. There's no point in worrying about what's to come. We should love each other regardless of heaven and hell's potential existence.

• I love Buddhism because it's simple and straightforward. It makes so much sense to me. I feel its veracity in my soul.

• Material things are superficial; you don't need them to be happy.

• Praying is not my thing. I believe in respecting the universe, but what is going to

happen is going to happen. It's about dealing with it, not asking for what you want to happen. It's about action and changing things by your own will, not pleading with an invisible man to take action for you.*

• Live in this moment, live now, live here.

• Find yourself. You aren't your job and your clothes. You're not your car and you're not a label you place yourself under. Strip everything away and what's left?

• Purification is liberating. I want to be a liberator.

• Everything in moderation; too much of anything is bad.

I am the liberator.

[*Ana: You're right, it's about you taking action rather than hoping some god will do the work for you. But the power of ritual and prayer is real, you just have to do it the right way. I couldn't honestly deny the fact that I've seen many physical manifestations of Saturn after I meet with him frequently during his day and/or hour and offer him appropriate gifts. Energy frequencies speak to you if you know how to contact them and recognize them in this dimension. Research astrological magic. You'll start to see that you can influence how energy manifests itself. You can call out to the Void and It will answer you. –J.]

08 February 2010

On Friday we took the new soccer recruits to this cafe that always has live music to see Kan's sister's fiancé play the guitar and sing. It was pretty neat.

At one point my whole leg fell asleep because of the position I was sitting in, but in such a way that I didn't really notice; it just felt like it needed to be stretched. When I stood up I fell kind of, like, collapsed, and everyone on the team laughed at me and I was embarrassed because we were right in front of everyone at the cafe. I could tell my face got super red.

Then we went to Adin's and I got drunk with Kan and the sophomores on our team. It was a small party so we didn't stay long. Kan spent the night with Adin. I tried to make her leave but she wanted to stay so I was like, "Okay, whatever, I hope you don't regret this in the morning…"

On Saturday we went downtown and took the recruits to Pike's, and it was a lot of fun! I talked to people, people selling stuff at the booths, people I didn't know. It was revolutionary. It is making me less and less anxious.

That night we got shwasted at the sophomore girls' apartments. I smoked a cig on the roof, and then Kan and I climbed on top of this tower and peed on the cement, and looked out at Seattle. It was beautiful. So right.

She was upset about her mind, and we talked about important stuff, like her thing with Drake that she had, and about being depressed and anxious. I told her that she was the little dark speck in the corner in the stairway, and that she is beautiful because of it, and that she is everything; we all are.

09 February 2010

I've been in a kind of irritable mood lately. Yesterday in my dorm Natalie was being extremely annoying! She talks incessantly and plays stupid music and I seriously wanted to strangle her. Her and Lillian would not shut up when I was trying to go to sleep. Usually I can handle this pretty well.

Like, it's not that big of a deal, I can just put in headphones. But this time I wanted to scream. I have an incredible amount of self-control though, it's fucking crazy.

I don't want to care about other people's opinions and perceptions of me. I am a person without a culture. Is that false? I say things that I think are true and they aren't. I dunno why I say the things I do. What else needs to be said? There are questions regarding my existence that have gone unanswered. I'm confused about a lot of things. I am anxious and frustrated about my identity and my relationships with what exists and what doesn't.

I don't know how my mind is supposed to work, and if there even is a right or wrong regarding opinions and preferences. Emotions are hard to figure out. Right when I've decided I feel a certain way, it explodes in my face and then evaporates before I can see what happened.

I'm sensitive. I get strong vibes from varying sources. If so many things make me feel something different, how am I supposed to feel when I'm just me? What is "me"? I don't believe in anything. There is no strong meaning for me anywhere I can see. Don't ask me how I'm feeling. Am I making all of this up or do I actually feel it?

My issues are more existential than anything else. *Why* am I feeling certain things? *Who am I?* Afraid of *fear*, myself, what I'm capable of. Buddhism gets straight to the issue, not covering it up and letting it fester. What exactly are you afraid of? FEAR. That's what we're all really afraid of, is it not?

The most important thing is my mental health.

11 February 2010

Today's workout was at 6:45 a.m. It was hard but not as bad as it could have been. Cameron was pushing me; while we were sprinting she was like, "Stay with me, Ana!" And other stuff like that so I would go as hard as I could. I respect her so much. I seriously think she's the coolest person ever. Everything she does is fucking legit and awesome. I'm in love with her. If she were a lesbian and wanted to date me, I would do it. And I am not kidding, which is the funny part.

12 February 2010

Hypocrisy, because opposites are the same and there are exceptions to every rule.

I'm in Foundations and it's stimulating all this scrambled inspired controversy in my mind. How can we ever know for sure that any of this is real or matters? How can we know what's right and wrong?

At this point, my belief in Jesus is completely irrelevant, because what he teaches is how to love and be kind. Other people teach that as well…Gandhi, Buddha…I embrace all people because I see myself in them. I see the universe in them and I know how important that is. Unity.

I don't like to reduce the inner workings of my mind to any definition, any religion serving as a description of who I am. The closest I can come to doing that is deciding to be Buddhist, which I want to do, but at the same time I don't blindly accept everything they believe.

I've never been good at participating or following the crowd. There's always been this seed of rebellion growing inside me, teaching me to question everything and to find my own way, without an authority figure standing over me telling me what is right and wrong.

I don't believe in an afterlife, in a heaven or hell, because I need proof of its existence. I picture ideas of the afterlife as a kind of reassurance that this life is meaningful for people who are afraid to live. It also seems to serve as a reason to refrain from misbehavior, which doesn't get to the root of why the misbehavior has occurred, or misbehavior's inherent nature, which seems important to understand psychologically.

Christianity is too concerned with the afterlife, and I don't understand how that is relevant right now. Right *now*, as I'm writing this, in this moment. It really is quite insignificant. Also, they speak of love and accepting each other, and it makes sense, but they don't act on it! They're judgmental and say harsh things. (Of course it's not all of them.)

I just want to separate myself from their drama. I see the way they are feeling and I think it's cute kind of, how agitated and irritated they get. You know, the whole "accept Jesus or burn in hell" mindset. Or that if you're gay you're automatically going to hell. Some people are so ignorant of the world and what truly matters. I'm not saying I'm perfect, but I am working on it.

I'm working on loving people and having a peaceful mind. I'm working on this because it is truth, and I need truth. Not because Jesus tells me I should feel this. I want to do nice things to people because I feel like it, not because everyone says I should or that it's the right thing to do.

I respect to the utmost extent the Christian perspective, and every other religious viewpoint, as well, just not the perverted versions of them where they say that men can do whatever they want but women's behavior should be super restricted, or that particular races are inferior to others.

It disappoints me when the respect I show is not reflected in other people's eyes. I also feel sad when they try to convert me, because this means that they do not understand my humanity. Why must I be converted in order to be valued? They can't find themselves in me, or see their reflection in a lake on a summer morning and think of me and how we're all connected.

I don't need God as defined by Christian terms to lead a beautiful and fulfilling life. I need love, nature, and people who accept me. I need knowledge and truth and peace, and I want to find these things on my own. If they are forced upon me I will always reject them.

My nails are getting longer. I don't bite them anymore because my anxiety isn't as prevalent. I think this is cool, and when I say cool I mean healthy. I'm in a good mood. I appreciate this pencil I am writing with and the coffee I have almost finished. I appreciate Foundations because it makes me understand what I believe, and how simple it actually is.

15 February 2010

Today I went downtown with Kan and we stole a *shit*-ton of shit. Old Navy, Gap, Sephora. It was ridiculous and surprisingly easy. We went to Ballard and were walking around as it was getting dark. The sky morphed from light blue and pink to navy and violet, and the lights from the boats in the water were brilliant, each a siren piercing through me. We smoked cigarettes as rebellion and drank coffee all day.

Yesterday was Valentine's Day and I rearranged our dorm. Jean helped me after a while. I've decided I like her a lot. She has a dry sense of humor and is also really good at drawing! Maybe she only seems so good because I am extremely bad at drawing.

Today when Lillian got back she changed our room a bit as well, and now it looks amazing. I feel excited because it's like I have my own room since it's the way I want it to be. My mattress is on the floor now instead of the top bunk. No more climbing awkwardly over my desk!

I feel like a real person lately! I live in Seattle, I ride the bus downtown and spend my days shoplifting, people watching, and letting the scent of coffee and cigarettes permeate my skin. It's lovely.

This past weekend we went to Adin's house. I drank, got real tipsy but probably not drunk. It was fun. Mariah got *super* shwasted and was throwing up. Sierra and I took care of her and I felt like a good friend, which I think I was.

Trevor was flirting with me and it made me really weird. Him and Mila have a fucked up relationship. He grabbed me around the waist and pulled me over so I was sitting on him, and then when Kan came in the room I was like, "Kan!" I got up to go over to her and he just kept grabbing me and pulling me back over to him, and it happened, like, four times. I said, "You are mean for keeping me from my best friend!" When he finally let me go he said, "I was jealous!"

I am totally in love with him. He has the same emotional and artistic mind as I do, and I find his body and face very attractive. And it's *not* okay, absolutely never permitted *ever*, because I adore Mila and she is clearly in love with him, and they are basically in an exclusive relationship! So weird, he gives me weird messages.

18 February 2010

I'm supposed to be writing my "credo" for my Foundations class, which is what I believe, who I am, basically. But how

83

the fuck am I supposed to do this if I don't know who I am? I'm so confused right now. At least it's due in March. March first, to be precise, so I have a couple weeks. But, still, it's making me anxious, which is not a big deal because I can kind of handle my anxiety now that I'm taking Zoloft.

I don't know what the truth is about reality. And what is going on, and what I'm thinking, and what is right and wrong. I feel like I'm supposed to be feeling a certain way, like I'm supposed to be happy, but am I happy? I don't know. Do I want to be happy if I'm supposed to be happy? I've spent my whole life doing what everyone is not doing, because I don't know why. I don't want to be happy if people tell me that is what I should do.

I don't know why I have never wanted to follow the crowd. Why do I want to be separate? Why do I want to be an individual?* I feel like it is good to be unique, it gives me good vibes, vibes of importance. I feel lovely when I'm not the same, but sometimes I feel like somehow it's wrong to be separate.

I've been reading a ton of Buddhist stuff, and a lot of it makes so much sense to me, but at the same time I get confused because I think about it too much. I think that what they say applies to all situations when it sort of does, but not really. For example: stealing. I think Buddha said something about not stealing, but at the same time I feel free when I do it. I feel like it makes me less materialistic and it stimulates my brain, heightens my fear and anxiety, which I need to learn to deal with.

I don't know. It gives me a rush and I feel like I know the consequences and I will accept the trouble I get in if I get into any. I want bad things to happen to me sometimes. I need to deal with things because I feel like I've never dealt with anything big. I feel like if I accept the consequences then I'm allowed to do it. Well, not legally allowed to do it, obviously. It's the psychological rationalization of the feeling triggered by the action of stealing that seems to matter.

I understand that things don't matter, that what matters is in your mind, like loving and connecting with other people. If I have to go to jail and pay a fine, then whatever, I'll do it. It's what I feel when I do it that is important. I'm stealing to feel something in particular, not only to steal. I don't truly *need* any of the things I steal, so if I end up losing them or they get stolen from me then whatever, it's fine, because it was never mine in the first place. In this way I feel it makes me less materialistic.

I want to do bad things because of this, but also I want to *not* want to do them, but not because they are "bad," but because I just don't feel like doing them. Does this make any sense? I don't want to refrain from stealing because an authority figure tells me I should. I want to refrain from stealing because I want to. I want to get to this point psychologically, but I'm not there yet.

Back to the Buddhism thing. I want to clear my mind and get rid of all these thoughts sometimes. I can do that by zazen, which is meditation. Buddhism is not about some god that is telling me what to do or what is right and wrong, which I think is important. It's about truth and finding the truth on your own. But it still makes me feel wary when they are like, you *have* to do zazen or nothing will happen, you will be clouded by delusion.

Now I imagine that right now I'm a monster, consumed by delusion and all my words are just crowding my brain and keeping me from reality and truth. I really don't want this to happen! I feel like I'm doing everything wrong. There are too many thoughts and I get them out on paper like this, but then I feel like that is bad because my brain generates more thoughts.

I'm sure Buddhists wouldn't say words are bad, but maybe I need a little bit more quiet mind time. Maybe I've been rambling my whole life and now I need to get my rambling and quiet mind time closer to moderation. They need to be balanced.

I need more balance in my life. I am searching for peace, calm, truth, reality. They are all right here, right now, but I need to feel it in my mind. I need to sense it. I can't because there are so many things running through my head that confuse me and I don't know how to act or what to do or who I am. It's frustrating and kind of scary. But, I dunno if it's scary.

I feel sad, disappointed. But the fact that I feel sad and lost in itself makes me real, makes me a person. I need to be happy that I'm feeling something. That's why I wrote the lyrics to "Zero" by the Smashing Pumpkins on those white shoes I had in high school. Because Billy Corgan had it right. I'm in love with the fact that I can feel sadness and that I am feeling something right now.

It's weird because already I'm feeling better, just because I said that. It's the Zoloft, I swear it is. Before I started taking it, this whole thought process would have put me in a deep depression, but now I worked myself out of it, and I'm okay, I think.

I think I know the way to the truth, but I'm not sure if it's actually the way to the truth, rather than a trick, rather than another bullshit religion about God and heaven and hell. I am hesitant because I want it to be right and I don't know if it is.

Maybe I need to do things I don't want to do. I don't want to do zazen because it scares me, because I'm afraid of what will happen, afraid of my mind. I am afraid of what won't happen. I'm afraid it will be wrong, but I need to let myself go and try it and quit making excuses.

This is really important right now. I think I've got something here. I think in my credo I'm going to talk about how I'm searching for truth, and how I think I know the way to the truth, but I have to work on it. I have to give myself up and become vulnerable to something in order to find out who I am. Because I've never truly given myself up to anything before.

I'll say that I've never had any huge traumas that have changed my life and made me believe in any certain thing. Buddhism just sounded the most correct to me. It cleared away all the bullshit about authority figures making rules and commandments, and cut straight to the core of my issues about my existence. About what I'm doing and what reality is and why I'm here.

I'm going to give myself up to zazen. I'm going to believe in something because I need it. I need something to hold on to, and I don't know why. I don't even know if that's true or if I just made it up right now. Zazen might not lead to the truth, but I shouldn't worry about it.

In any case, it can't be bad for my mental health. Quieting your mind is definitely good for one's sanity and the least I can do is try it. As for getting a zen master to guide me, we'll see how that works out. I might need some help with that.

[*Ana: It's because you're Aquarius rising and Saturn is conjunct your Sun and North Node in his own sign of Capricorn. Saturn is your cosmic overlord. –J.]

I want to be street smart. I hate being afraid of the people downtown, which is where I am now. I'm going to start coming here often so my fear fades away. It's almost ten at night. I have to catch the bus.

I've doubted myself and that's why I needed Buddhism to tell me that I don't need to follow any rules or obey a god to be happy and to find peace. It told me that everything is okay, that I'm real and wonderful and that I don't need to worry. I turned to Buddhism rather than real people because I was never able to ask for help from people. I have too much pride, and it's fucking strange! I was always independent, always on my own, happy being by myself, so when Buddhism told me to find truth by following my own path, I embraced this wholly, because it made sense to me.

I'm afraid of not having control over myself, does that mean I value myself?

I want to transcend my opinions and desires.

If someone's happy, why do you have to try to change them, convert them?

There's no good and bad, there's just action! That's why when I steal I don't feel guilty, because it's more about the feeling. It's more about being free from the constraints of society.

I'm afraid of disagreeing with truth. I'm afraid that Buddhism is ultimate truth and that if I don't do what they say I'll be wrong. Well, so fucking what? If I'm wrong I'll realize it and I'll go a different way. I shouldn't be afraid of anything, I should go my own way! I should try things out, it's okay if I'm wrong because I'll figure it out.

Am I afraid of failure?

Yesterday Kan and I ran around Gasworks, which was mesmerizing. For the past couple of days it's been bright and sunny and kind of warm, and completely clear! It's weird. It makes me feel like I'm at home because the weather is how Boise weather would be.

We went downtown and hung out at Pike's for two or three hours, sitting on these stairs and talking to the guys that hand out the Fuji apple samples. I'm in love with one of them; his name is John and he has a blonde mustache and wears a hat that says Norway on it.

23 February 2010

Kan and I went downtown again and went to our same spot and ate Fuji apples. We figured out that John has a girlfriend, nooo! We shoplifted a bit as well. We got matching Starbucks mugs, and I got two eyeliners and a Butterfinger from Walgreens and two hair clips from the Westlake mall.

On Monday I had class and I went on a run and volunteered at the Union Gospel Mission. Volunteering was for my psychology class, but I also used it as community service for when River and I got in trouble for trying to sleep in the empty apartment at the guys' complex. I'm happy I was able to make that work for both things; it made me feel very efficient.

27 February 2010

Yesterday Kan, her friend Lauren, Lauren's best friend

Hailey, and I went to a party in UW, and it was so much fun! Way more fun than the parties here. I didn't even get all the way drunk and I still had fun.

I met this guy who had a ton of cool books in his room, including *The Singularity is Near: When Humans Transcend Biology*, the book Sawyer and Dad are obsessed with, and the one I wish I was smart enough to fully comprehend but sounds interesting anyway. He had a lot of philosophy books as well and we talked about ethics and cooking.

Yesterday we had a soccer meeting and then ate Thai food as a team. I got tofu delight and it was tasteless. That's okay, I guess, because I stole the little bowl my rice came in and now I use it as a bracelet holder. My kleptomania is actually getting a little out of hand. It's such an addiction. Every time I walk into a store I look for the cameras and think about the best way to steal something.

On Wednesday Kan and I went downtown with the intent to do homework, which was a big, fat fail! We went to Macy's and tried to steal stuff, but we chickened out because this guy kept following us around everywhere and I decided that he probably was a security guard.

I'm feeling a lot of things. First of all, I feel kind of sad because the UW party was so cool, and I feel like if I went to a huge public college I would have more fun and meet more people that understand me. Or at least people that have the same interests as me, or that aren't obsessed with Jesus. I feel like I don't belong here and it sucks.

Then, I feel weird kinda because talking to people is no longer something that freaks me out and makes me anxious, and I dunno if that's good or bad. I feel like I'm not being me. But, at the same time, I think I enjoy not having to avoid people because of my anxiety. I don't know, it's just an idea/feeling that I'm struggling with in my head a bit.

01 March 2010

I can follow Jesus as a good example, but I don't need him to be my savior. When dealing with trauma I don't need to think or feel that he is watching over me, because I don't believe he is. It's illogical to think that, and its only purpose is to give you peace of mind, when you should generate that with your own willpower.

Try to let go of everything - God, materials, desires. Live now. When you're high, be high. Don't try to get away from it because it won't happen, it'll make it worse. Embrace the mindset you're in, rather than worrying about it. Love every-thing about yourself, right *now*. Your mind is what you struggle with, not the world. Not life. It's how you feel and perceive outside stimuli that fucks you up.

07 March 2010

Today Natalie and I went to the Fremont Sunday market. Yesterday we went to Pike's and to the waterfront, and it was nice. I am liking her more and more, it's good. Right now we are watching the Academy Awards, and I haven't seen any of these movies they are talking about. Ugh.

A week and a half till spring break. So excited. I've been reading Natalie's manga series, *The Queen's Knight*. Rieno is sexy.

I dyed part of my hair orange, where the blue was that had faded. It looks legit.

Problems, and dealing with them:

I never knew if what I was feeling was normal or not, and now I am wondering if that even matters. Why should I be normal? I should just be myself. I want things to be okay, I suppose.

For the past few years I've been living in my room, letting people make me anxious, being too afraid to go do things, not living, not being happy. I was not being happy because I was too busy trying not to be anxious. Things made me feel bad so I spent my life avoiding them.

Now I am trying to deal with life by living and I'm realizing that things don't really scare me, make me anxious anymore, but I forget and start avoiding them when I don't need to. I am trying to ease my way into doing things that used to make me feel bad. Sometimes they still make me feel bad, but not nearly as much, so it's still kind of hard to do them. I feel sad because I've been wasting my life and I feel like I still am sometimes.

I'm still trying to deal with my existence. Everything is so crazy, so strange. I feel like the fact that I have a mind, a tool used to interpret outside stimuli – the world – is fucking weird, and I feel insane when I think about it too much. There are vibes everywhere, and knowing that other people feel differently about things, and feel different vibes coming from the same stimulus, is hard to think about.

People don't understand a lot of the time, especially about religion, and that's frustrating. It's super frustrating because they think they've found the ultimate truth so they disregard differing perspectives. They ignore how it's definitely possible that their truth *couldn't* be the truth for someone else. I feel like what they believe isn't truth. If you're homosexual you go to hell, how can that be truth? How could anyone ever think that is right?

I feel like I know where I can find truth, I only have to work on it. Is there one Absolute Truth? To my mind, perceptions, rationality, and ideas of fairness? Who the fuck am I? And why can't I figure this shit out? Why is this so important?

You know how you feel when you see someone and you want to be exactly like them? And they look intriguing and refreshing? I want to feel that way about myself but it's hard. I want people to get it but I won't let anyone get it. I don't let people in.

I don't want to be ignorant or apathetic. I'm trying to find wisdom and truth and an open mind, and happiness, I suppose.

Bad things have happened to the people that end up being homeless or "crazy" and the way they have dealt with these things has placed them into the position they are in. I shouldn't judge them or consider myself better than them because I could have turned out exactly like them if the same things had happened to me. There is no need to think that either myself or those people are stronger or weaker than the other, because there is no need for comparison or competition. There is no need to judge because I am not in that position and I do not understand the situation.

When you do something, really do it. When you feel anxious, do something. Cut yourself, say something bad to someone, cry, hold your breath, yell off the balcony, run. Don't stay in your head, it's not healthy. It's bad, makes it worse. Wherever you go, you are in the right place; you're here, now.

How do we know that we are being honest with ourselves?

13 March 2010

Saturday. Today all I did was run around Gasworks, study, and eat. It was good, though. Gasworks was liberating, as usual. It was sunny and windy, and people were flying kites and everyone was happy. The water was moving with the wind and there were multiple sailboats. I was listening to White Lies, and it was lovely. Everything was good.

Yesterday was the last normal day of classes. I studied Psych all day and felt fat. I had a Psych test yesterday as well, and I got a 42 out of 45. Boo fucking yah.

Finals are on Monday and Tuesday, and my flight home is also on Tuesday. I am excited to go home! Last Thursday we had practice and I played well. Chadwick was happy. He told me I had a great week. I am starting to like soccer again, it's marvelous and strange. I feel my confidence sprouting.

14 March 2010

Today I went to the art center on campus with Jean and Lillian and studied all day. It was quiet and spacious and lovely. We drew Hello Kitty as a zombie on the white board in the room we were in, and this guy walked in and saw it and stopped to contemplate it before leaving. We could barely stifle our laughter, it was funny.

My mentality is much better lately; I haven't felt depressed in what seems like a long time. And when something bad does happen, I embrace it because it makes me feel real. It's weird, I just have such a better outlook on life.

I have come to realize that even when I was depressed, it was

94

beautiful because it was real, and I dunno. I think I always knew it was beautiful, but I couldn't feel happy about it, for obvious reasons. I was so fucking worried about everything; I could never relax, I could never like people. Now things are okay. I don't worry about shit that doesn't matter.

20 March 2010

I'm home, finally! Finals are over. All I know is that I got an A in Psych and I'm real happy. Also, Camila is here. Right now we are hanging out in a bookstore. Tomorrow we are going back to Lewiston to drop her off and visit Grandma in the hospital. I think I'm going to visit Camila's sorority house.

Recently I cleaned out my room, sold a ton of clothes to some recycled fashion stores, gave a ton of stuff to charity, and put a ton of stuff in storage. It felt good to purge.

Last night I had weird dreams. One was that I had sex with Calvin. *Bad.* I woke up feeling creepy and gross. And I never want to have sex.

25 March 2010

I want to get a yin yang tattoo on my arm, near my wrist. I was anxious today for no reason. There are too many things to say and I'm real tired. I need balance. Hence the tattoo.

• Scared to live, to fuck up, to hit bottom.

• Can't be perfect because it's impossible.

• Be nice to yourself. Don't be so critical.

• Have confidence. You can do what you aim to do. Life is a struggle but you are a strong person.

• No fucking fear! Don't let it take control!

• There is no self. There is only an ever-changing flux of emotions, habits, knowledge, and preferences.

Balance is comprehending the notion that nothing has only one side to it. Everything is connected because we are all everything. The potential to be anything resides within us. I am neither strong nor weak. I am a mixture of both in different situations.

I want that tattoo, but then I get this bad feeling that I'm doing the wrong thing, and I hate that! I hate that fucking feeling. I'm a real person, I can make my own decisions. Besides, it stands for a fundamental concept in life that I need to remember for my own sake.

27 March 2010

I have some things to say. I haven't felt like writing lately, but right now it feels like it's what I'm supposed to be doing. That last entry was me dealing with some random anxiety. Weird. All day on the 25th I worried.

Anyway, yesterday was better. I went on a run and then Mom and I went shopping and I stole some stuff. A lip balm, perfume, soap, underwear, and two unicorn keychains from the grocery store by our house, and I think that's it. But holy shit it is easy to steal shit! Just take everything into the dressing room. Jesus Christ. It was strange though, because I started to feel a bit bad, and I never feel bad! Also, Mom bought me this long, beachy dress and I'm so excited to wear it!

Oh, I just thought of something random. Living here and now means not basing who I am on the past. Of course my past affects who I am in the present, but I am a different person now. I'm a different person from who I was yesterday, and I think this is an important concept.

Yesterday I visited my grandpa on Dad's side at the old people home with Dad, and I basically played with this puppy that was there for the whole time. Also, I hung out with Eli and he can finally fucking drive now! Haha. It's nice to not have to pick him up.

I visited Camila's sorority when we went to Lewiston. I slept over there and it was fun, but I definitely would hate to live there. They all sleep in the same room. Gross. In the middle of the night this drunk girl came in and passed out in the bed right next to me, and she was hiccupping/heaving/gagging, and it was revolting. I thought she was going to vomit on me.

I'm really glad I don't live in a sorority. You have to conform to all their stupid little rules, and you have to hang out with annoying, dramatic girls. It sounds terrible to me.

Sawyer and I also hung out a lot in Lewiston. We climbed the mountain with the huge white C painted on it. It took forever but it was worth it to be so high up and see all of Lewiston and Clarkston. We saw these cows while hiking and they seemed like they wanted to charge us, it was scary. I think they wanted to mate and were being all weird and defensive.

On the drive home we dropped Sawyer off in McCall, as he is still working as a ski instructor there. It was good to talk to him and Mom. I love my family so much. It's fucking crazy to me how lucky I am to have them. It makes me happy.

Lately I've been realizing that I am a real person and I can do whatever the fuck I want. Like I can get a tattoo, and pierce my nose, or whatever! It's actually starting to hit me, and I am realizing that I need to do what makes me happy, not what pleases other people.

29 March 2010

I got arrested for shoplifting today at the mall. Embarrassing. I was with Mom so it was even worse. I feel like an idiot, kind of. I took two skirts into the dressing room and put them in my bag, and then bought a different skirt that was a lot cheaper.

Mom and I went to the bathroom outside of the store, and when we came out there was a lady standing there that said to me, "I'm with security, you have to come with me," and in my mind I was like, "Shiiiiit."* My mom hissed at me, "Did you take something?!" I had to tell her yes because it was obvious! They took me into this back room and questioned me and opened my bag to reveal the skirts, and it was awkward and uncomfortable.

Mom was freaking out, but I was calm and cooperative and I am proud of my reaction. I did not let them scare me when they were obviously trying hard to. I didn't freak out in my head, either. I think it is rational to be calm and accept one's punishment. I dunno, I think it's interesting when criminals act all self-righteous and like they weren't doing anything wrong when clearly they were. I will accept the consequences because I know what I did was a crime. It makes sense.

It just sucks that I got caught. Haha. It's inconvenient. I have to go to court in April. Even though this sucks I am kind of glad that I can say I have been arrested. And not for stupid shit like underage drinking. It adds to my list of experiences you know? Balance. Everything in moderation. Just kidding. Kind of.

It's strange because I totally had this terrible feeling like I knew I was going to get caught, but I did it anyway. I dunno why! I didn't follow my heart. When Kan and I were at Macy's in Seattle I got the same feeling and I followed it. This time I didn't. This is good because it taught me to follow my gut feelings, and the consequences weren't even that bad. I didn't have to spend the night in jail or anything, although I did have to go to jail. I had to take out all my piercings and they went through my bag and put all my stuff in plastic bags, which was annoying. But it was only one day, not a lifetime or even a year.

I realized that being in jail would be awful. When I was in there this lady was on the phone with someone, and she was crying because she got sentenced to ten years in jail. Isn't that terrifying? I felt bad for her, and at the same time relieved that I don't have to do that. So I guess I am planning on not getting arrested again. Try anything once, not twice. Ha.

Anyway, I'm a little embarrassed and it's an interesting feeling. I'll get over it. Mom was really mad at me and was like, "What were you thinking?!" Dad was not even mad or anything, he just seemed strangely amused. Like, I was in my room organizing the contents of my purse after the people at the jail scrambled everything, and he came in and said, "Don't you know they have cameras everywhere? *Everywhere.*" And that's all he said about it.

I think Sawyer and I are going to see *Avatar* at 9:55 tonight. Yesterday Dad and I saw *Legion* and it was corny but I thought it was kind of good. The main guy was immensely attractive to me.

[*Ana: In reality, you probably could have refused to go with her and suffered no consequences other than confused ques-

tioning by your mom. They can't grab you and drag you to
the back room with them. —J.]

03 April 2010

There are a lot of things to say. I'm back in Seattle for the
next quarter of school. Firstly, I'm irritated with Kan. It's
probably because I've been with her too much and I'm on my
period. She slept over last night, and I felt sick so I slept in
Lillian's bed because she was gone, when all I wanted in the
world was to be alone and sleep in my own bed because it's
relaxing. But no.

And she ate so much of my Nutella. This irritates the fuck out
of me because it's mine, you know? And I want to eat it, too!
I don't care if she eats it, but when she eats, like, 20 spoon-
fuls of it in a row and isn't even putting it on a bagel or something, that pisses me off. The fact that I get pissed because of
this makes me even more pissed because I know that it's
stupid and it doesn't matter and it's not that big of a deal. I
didn't freak out on her or anything, so I'm glad.

Also, I've been worried about soccer. On Thursday we had
practice and I did okay, but not that great, and it was frustrating and made me anxious. I really, *really* don't want last
season to happen to me again. Because it sucked so fucking
much. It for real was the worst year of my life. It's just
extremely irritating that I try so fucking hard and I still can't
play to my potential. It is the most frustrating, confusing,
embarrassing situation in the entire universe.

It's like those dreams you have when you're trying to punch
someone and no matter how hard you try you barely touch
them at all. You are so angry that the only thing that would
make it better is if they would die at your hands, but it never

happens. Or those dreams where someone is chasing you and you try to run away as fast as you can but it's like you are running in waist-deep water or that you have heavy weights on your legs that make it so that you can barely pick up your feet. Ugh. No one knows how I can play, and even I am starting to forget. It's depressing.

And Kan: SHE IS EXTREMELY FUCKING CRITICAL. Aahh! It's hard to ignore. She is so incredibly great at acting like she is so incredibly great at soccer, and saying little things about me and acting like she knows how I play, which she knows nothing about because I have not played to my potential since I've been here.

When I play I keep thinking about what she is thinking of me and about how I'm playing and it fucks me up and I play even worse. It's hard to forget about, but I'm trying. I need to forget her, I need to disregard her opinions because all that matters is what I think. It's about me, not her.

She also makes me feel like the way I deal with things is wrong, or that when I don't want to do something, the way I am feeling is stupid and I should just "get over it." Like, she wanted to go play soccer with the guys the other day, and I didn't want to, and she asked me why. I said I get bad vibes from it and you know what she said? "Oh my god, get over yourself! That's your ego talking." Can you fucking believe that? It really hurt me. You don't say that to people, it's just not something you do.

I try to think objectively about the matter whenever she says stuff like this, because maybe I am wrong, you know? But it's like, I don't want to do things that I don't want to do! I think I get bad vibes from it because I'm still trying to like soccer again. They are guys and much better, so I'll probably end up feeling stupid, and I'm still self-conscious.

She doesn't understand that I'm not perfect and that she isn't perfect either, and that I don't have to live up to any of her fucking standards, and I don't have to like the same things she likes. That's not my thing, playing with the guys. I don't like it. It's going to take time for me to enjoy soccer again, so I need to take it slow and feel okay with it when it's happening.

I feel like I'm learning things about myself. Like, I need my fucking space, and I am neat and tidy and I'm good at sharing, but it is possible for people to take advantage of that and it makes me angry. I also have realized that I don't like confrontation, because people are naturally defensive and can't truly understand how I feel, and I don't like when people are angry.

I am not the most mentally strong person because I am sensitive and feel a lot and often take things personally, but at least I realize this and can try to be better. People are just inconsiderate though, and completely disregard how you're feeling. This is why I hate people! No one understands and not many of them care. It's ridiculous.

So this is what I'm going to do: love myself, have confidence. Love the way I do things and don't listen to anyone else. Obviously I need to listen to them, but never feel that I am inadequate. Never let anyone tell you that you can't do something.

04 April 2010

I never told you that we went to the Owl City concert. I cried the whole time because it was so meaningful to me. I felt unity in that moment, and I felt like things would be okay and that people cared about me, and I remembered running by

Gasworks and hearing the "Hello Seattle" remix right when I saw the city. That moment was important for some reason and I'll never forget it.

Right now everything is still and quiet; everyone is gone for Easter. I ran yesterday and it was really nice. I also went to the Sounders game with Hope and Bridgette. They lost but I didn't care. It was my first time going to one of those games so it was an adventure. Chadwick gave us tickets because we were the only ones on the team in Seattle for Easter and we didn't have anything to do.

I feel good today. The silence on the weekends used to be oppressive, but it's soothing right now. I am trying to do what I would do if I were at home. It's comforting and it feels safe. Because at home I'm usually alone and I like it a lot. It's better there because I have a whole house to do activities in, and here it's only one room, which sucks.

Last night I hung out with Zara for a bit and watched *The Ugly Truth*. I also downloaded the new Gorillaz album, *Plastic Beach*, and put some pics from my fisheye camera on Facebook. I think I'll go read now.

05 April 2010

We're reading *My Name is Asher Lev* in one of my classes and I adore it. I wish I could be more like Asher. He knows what he loves and he feels things without worrying about it. Kinda. He's real. He's who I want to be when I'm hating myself and my lack of artistic talent.

Where do those moments come from? When you feel that things are important, and there is something else there but you can never define it. Like when it rains at night and the wind is shaking the trees and the lights are dim because of the mist. You feel safe, hidden wherever you are, in your big armchair with the faded red fabric. You've had it for years and you'll never dispose of it.

These words have never been said, you think. Because of that you feel that you are the single most important being in existence, and that somehow your creativity justifies your breathing.

You take a swig of the tea you've prepared, and feel happy that it's storming and dark, because of that thing, that thing that's indefinable and its existence is questionable and you know it's not God because you don't believe in God. But it makes you feel good, like how you imagine you'd feel if you were the people in the books you consume, or the voices in the music you love. As if you could feel nothing and everything, eating you from the inside out.

Eat words, digest whole paragraphs, regurgitate meaning. It's probably meaning, captured from everything you value and stored in those books that are really you, tucked behind your father's ear, hidden underneath the soil where you buried the body. All you've ever wanted is meaning, where is it? Where? It's everything anyone has ever felt. Art is everything you touch. It is dirty and disgusting. Those are gagging sounds, but it's still beautiful.

Everything is everything. We're all insane.

11 April 2010

Last night we went to a party at the Jungle and I got the most drunk I have ever been, ever. Ugh. I made out with this random junior named Chris and my bottom lip is bluish now from him biting me. I think it's hilarious.

I threw up a bit. I actually made myself because I knew I would feel better afterwards, and I was right. Kan and I slept on the futon at the Jungle because I could *not* make it back to my dorm. This morning we walked back to campus and it was beautiful outside! Warmish and sunny and breezy. Today basically all I did was get over my hangover.

On Wednesday it was Mariah and Cameron's birthdays, so we went to this Italian restaurant and I ate the most I have ever eaten in one sitting. It was bad. We all wore black because Cameron was depressed that she is getting older, so we acted like it was a funeral.

On Thursday my design class, which is about architectural and interior design, met at the public library downtown and took a small tour, it was sweet. I walked around there for a while afterwards because I had nothing to do and didn't have to be back on campus.

On Friday Natalie and Lillian and I went to the Northgate mall and I bought some shirts and this amazing Hello Kitty backpack, and Mad Libs and Hello Kitty bows for my hair. Fresh!

We had a game on Saturday and lost. We hit the crossbar, like, ten times though. I played all right. Not amazing by any means, but not terrible either. I felt tired and nervous. Ah well, I'll get over it. I feel a lot better now that I'm so Zolofty.

13 April 2010

Today I had weight room at 8:30 a.m. and class at 10:30 a.m. Now I'm at a coffee shop downtown with Kan. We've been walking around down here. There are so many people. I wonder about them, each body. Meaning is intricately wasted in infinite spasms of firing neurons. I want to know where they're all going. Why are there so many things about them that seem so important? It's pointless but it's all right. We're all selfish but somehow it's significant.

I wanted to have a flowing poetic entry, but this is a failure worthy of a magnificent display of disrespect. I'm a human, always a human first. It's confusing. Because we have existential struggles, we try to find purpose, direction, meaning. And I dunno if it's worth it. It sucks struggling through your own ideas, trudging through the layers of your own perception and getting lost in your own mind. But it *is* beautiful, it's fucking human and stupid and lovely and irritating and perfect.

I haven't been doing my own thing because I'm always around people. I'm trapped by soccer and a Christian school. Struggling to succeed. Weighed down by thoughts laced with poisonous anxiety. Why? Does everyone struggle to do well? It's annoying to me. It's fantastic to fail, isn't it? It's a paradox, a catch-22. The more you try to figure it out, the more you fail. The more lost you become.

No thinking. It's interesting how sometimes you can create something and hate it so much, and be critical of it, while other people find it fascinating. I want to start creating more things. I want to write more, read more. I want a vocabulary dripping with pandemonium.

14 April 2010

It's stifling here. Kan wants me to be things I'm not. I've slowly come to realize this. It's fucking weird to me. I should count the number of times she tells me I should do something, or how my beliefs are not being open to questioning and doubt.

If you become a part of something, rules and norms are always created. I dunno why. It irritates me. I don't want to be a part of anything. I want to do my own thing, and it's hard here. I'm cold, on the balcony lounge of my dorm. Maybe I do want to be a part of something. Something fucking important. I don't want to be stressed, though. Soccer makes me stressed. I'm working on it.

15 April 2010

Today practice was good. Every time it gets better, it's fucking good.

Kan, Eugenia, and I went dumpster diving for Anthropology. We learned in that class that you can tell a lot about a person, group, or culture from what they throw away. Eugenia is another girl on our team who is a year older and is one of our goalies. I've never had a class with her before so it's fun to interact with her in a different context. We stole a garbage bag full of doughnuts from this doughnut shop's dumpster on Queen Anne. They were perfectly good doughnuts!

Kan's been irritating me. Lately she has been making me feel like I'm not my own person, it sucks.

Tomorrow is Friday and no practice! Woo! Tonight I watched a million old music videos from the 90's, like Aaron Carter and Lil' Bow Wow. Hilarious.

I am okay. I dunno what to say. I want to be more myself, like do more things that I would do at home. I don't really have the resources, like Mom's advice or all the shit you can find in the drawers in the laundry room.

It's 1:20 a.m. I love the way this pen flows. These things are important. I want to get into music again. I haven't been and I don't like it because music helps me feel things. Okay I'm going to go to bed and listen to "Superfast Jellyfish" by Gorillaz. They make me feel.

16 April 2010

I hate being around all these people.

18 April 2010

We did this fundraiser the other day as a team for people in Africa, and it was way more fun than I imagined it would be. It was in this park with a path around a lake, and it was getting dark out. Cool breeze, deep colors fading in the shadows. Rain for a while, and the grayness that's always apparent afterwards.

Saturday was our game in Portland. My family came and it was nice. We won, like, 5-1 and I scored once. It wasn't that cool of a goal, though. Other than that, yesterday I didn't do much. I listened to music while we drove to and from Portland, and read *Salem's Lot* by Stephen King. It's all right, a quick read I think.

Today is Sunday and it's beautiful outside. Warmth, sun. It's hot actually, no clouds. I walked around Fremont alone and found a little park where I sat against a tree and read for a long while. I walked everywhere and didn't go into any of the shops because I don't want any more things.

I think I was meant to be alone. When I was reading against the tree there was this guy with dreads that lives in one of the houses there, and I kept seeing him everywhere, like driving around. I think he waved to me at one point, it was weird.

24 April 2010

I am drunk. Tonight was cool. I went to Adin's. I talked to Chris, the guy I made out with last time, and he totes wants me. He talked about how we got off on the wrong foot and I was like, "It's totally cool, like, it's fine, I really don't care about what happened last time." He kept staring at me, and everywhere I went he was in the background. It was weird. He's super awkward. Who is awkward when drunk? No one. Except him. I talked to Cameron a lot, too. She said she smokes mota every day, and I swear to god she's the coolest person I know.

Today I woke at 10:30 a.m., went back to bed at 12:30, and slept till four. What the fuck?

My past Ethics professor added me on Facebook. Oh my evolution, (we've started saying "oh my evolution" instead of "oh my god") he knows I exist. Crazy.

Tonight was weird. Before the party Jean curled my hair and Kan teased it hardcore. I don't feel that drunk but I know I am. It's almost three in the morning. I think I should go to bed. I'm going to wash my face. I can't believe I'm writing right now.

25 April 2010

I am in Starbucks in Fremont with Kan, Zara, Lillian, and Jean. We went to the market and bought a mota pumpkin bread thing, but we aren't going to eat it yet. There's this lady at the far end of the market that sells bongs, and she has a secret menu of mota things, it's awesome.

I want to say everything that needs to be said. Sometimes I feel so good, like everything will be all right, and it's all okay, like last night at the party. Sometimes that feeling evaporates and then I can only sense small traces of it, like the lingering scent of a person that has left the room moments before. I've been trying to capture that feeling and hold it because it makes me feel safe. I get glimpses of anxiety and it's discomforting. I can't figure out if I want to feel this way. Somehow it feels important, glorifying almost. All the famous, beautiful people have suffered. All the artists.

I feel like it makes me cute, vulnerable, lovely, fragile. Not in a feminine way, in a human way. In a way that demonstrates how insignificant we are compared to everything there is. It shows that we all balance each other out, kind of. Like, the great suffer, and the mundane are happy but unimportant, in a sense.

I am not an artist, in the world's definition, maybe. But, fuck the world. I am an artist at heart I think, but that's not enough. I wish I could be a legitimate artist, make a living artistically. Or have an artist boyfriend and make him do everything artsy while I read and drink coffee and smoke cigarettes all day and watch his mind unravel.

At the market today this guy started talking to me and he was the artist of one of the stands that make screen prints or something. I think he was on drugs, but he was cute.

The other day I went to the Henry Art Museum with Lillian, her boyfriend Al, and one of their random friends from UW, and it was so cool. There's this quiet room where you can go to study or whatever, and the lights are dim and welcoming.

There are also computers and books and magazines. I'm totes going to go to UW more often. It's so fucking cool. I wish I could go there instead of the Christian shit-hole I'm currently involved with.

The Henry Museum and the art project I'm supposed to be doing for my Core class, which is another required class like Foundations, has made me start thinking of all this artist stuff, and how I want to be an artist. And how I'm frustrated because I'm not an artist and I feel like the things I make are shit and worthless.

I wish I had good ideas, and I want my art project to be legit. I'm going to use the book that my brother made me with the pages cut out to hide things in. I still have to formulate some ideas, like, symbolically. Like what I'm trying to highlight about myself. I was thinking about doing my existential issues as a main theme, like questions I am confused about and how I wish I were the people in the books I read. And how I *am* those people; I'm exactly like them, but for some reason I can't feel this. So if I use the book to cradle my confusion about life, it will represent symbolically how I actually *am* in the books I read.

27 April 2010

Yesterday at practice I cried to Bailee, who is a year older and also plays in the midfield, and to Chadwick, because I was in the worst mood and I'm frustrated with the formation and how to defend correctly. Chadwick wants me to only follow the midfielder on the other team around and defend her the entire time. I don't want to do that, I just want to play! I don't want to focus on someone else the entire game, especially because I'm not a fucking defender! It's like he wants me to play in a very particular way that doesn't coincide with how a person should actually play when they're a midfielder and good at soccer. He won't let me be myself on the field.

He is so fucking persistent. I can't simply *not* try to play how he wants because he's the coach, and if I don't play how he wants then I will sit on the bench and not play at all. He bombards me with questions about why I didn't do a particular thing in a specific way, and it's really overwhelming, especially when it happens almost every practice. He interrogates me about why I wasn't following the other midfielder around the whole game like he asked, and it's heavy and depressing, because I'm not allowed to focus on myself and try to play well. I have to focus on someone else, and if I don't I get in trouble. And all of this makes me play even worse because I can't get into my flow state.

I try to think of all these ways to escape his interrogations. To defeat him, avoid him, head him off in a different direction, give him the wrong directions. Nothing is ever successful because his unrelenting, psychological, manipulative, negative energy is too strong. I know somehow it's safe to say that he tries to get in your head, and he tries persistently and over a long duration of time, so that it becomes an obstruction to mindfulness.

Today is safe because it's raining and I'm leaning against a wall in the corner of the coffee shop on campus out of everybody's way, and the lights are low and warm. I'm wearing sweats and I'm alone. Alone is so beautiful and so terrible. It's all I've ever wanted and everything that makes me hate who I am.

29 April 2010

How can I be rational in an insane world when I don't even know what rationality is anymore?

30 April 2010

So many fucking things. I am awkward. I never talk. I can't trust people. That's why I've been playing bad? I felt I couldn't trust them, I couldn't give them everything, I still can't give them everything. I don't open up to people. I hate this and I love it. I'm in love with my depression.

Yesterday at practice we had a huge talk because people were offended at the talk we had after our game. I felt good after it because I felt like people cared about me. I had to say my opinion and I was sooo awkward and my face turned bright red because I could feel them all staring at me. When Cameron talks she is very articulate. She knows everything and I'm in love with her.

There's this coffee shop in Capitol Hill called Bauhaus, and we went there last night because it's open till one in the morning, and I got all my homework done. It was Kan, Mila, Cameron, Eugenia, and me. I love hanging out with them even if we're only doing homework. There were tons of interesting people there, it was lovely and comforting.

The other day I was thinking about how fucking crazy it is that I exist at this moment. That right here, right now, I am alive. I was reading about killing babies for Anthropology (that sounds funny, but seriously) and I was thinking about how insane it is that I was born in the United States. I'm lucky to have been born here rather than a tiny third world country somewhere.* It's incredible that I'm not dead, that I've lived this far.

[*Ana: Yeah, you're lucky to have been born in the country

113

that does terrible things to other countries, rather than in the countries that have terrible things done to them. You should research what the USA has done to Central America, as a start, to show you how "lucky" you are. –J.]

03 May 2010

I forgot to tell you that we got high last Tuesday. We ate this pumpkin bread that we bought in Fremont from the lady at the market with the secret menu. Kan, Zara, and I. Kan was a huge bitch, I wasn't scared (weird!), and Zara was paranoid. It was legit. I wanna do it again. Zara and I watched *The Ring* later that night, and ate an entire bag of white cheddar Cheetos Puffs.

I want to say something. It is that I am here right now, and I'm constantly moving into the future and it's beautiful. And scary. Time is diminishing. It's cool because I can do whatever I want. I have this body that I get to be in charge of. Each day can be an adventure, and the only thing that gets in the way is my feelings about particular things. Sometimes I feel like I'm dealing with things wrong, that I'm not the people in the books. That I'm not real. Just this worry means that I am real, though. I don't have to be anything anyone tells me to be.

06 May 2010

I am drinking a hazelnut latte with soy milk and eating the free scone that came with it. It's Thursday, but no practice because yesterday was our last for spring season. I am real excited for freedom, it's going to be glorious.

Today was good. I had class and it went by relatively fast. I got all my homework done and then went downtown to the art museum since it's free on the first Thursday of every month. I also went to the library and it was calm and empty.

I was looking through the DVDs and I found *Science of Sleep* and *Paprika*! It was lucky, I can't even believe I found them. What a random coincidence, since I was thinking about *Paprika* just the other day. I love it.

I feel like everything has been working out today. Everyone kept looking at me, like more than usual. I am pretty used to people looking at me, but I swear every single person I saw looked at me like I was wearing something super strange or had something on my face, and neither of those things were true today.

This old Indian guy started talking to me at the bus stop and when I had to go he was like, "I love you!" And I was like, "Love ya too!" It was funny.

I had a small headache all day, it sucked. Except music made it feel better.

I kept getting glimpses of a feeling today. The feeling was that I was mysterious, and living on my own in Seattle. Un-tourist-like. I felt like I was calm, I knew what I was doing. And the thing is, I do know what I'm doing. Downtown Seattle is familiar. I know what bus to take, I know the streets and where everything is. I still can't believe I know these things.

My mind won't understand that I have acquainted myself with a main city in this country. It's big, bustling, scary, and I have tamed it. I wish I could have done this quicker, though. I feel like there are things I still need to experience, but I don't know what they are and I'm not a part of anything, so how will I come to know what I'm missing? I don't know, it's complicated.

Last night right after I finished reading for my class, Mila texted me and told me to come drink with them in the guys' apartments…so I did. Bailee let me have a few shots, legit. I ended up playing Mario with Drake and Max and Trevor. It was fun.

On Tuesday Mila and I visited the coffee shop Eugenia works at and stayed till it closed. Ed came eventually and we all went to Ethiopian food. We laughed so hard at so many things. I love hanging out with other people besides Kan. That sounds rude, maybe, but it's true. We've become too close and she thinks we're the same person, and doesn't understand when we have differing opinions. It's okay, though. I just need to see other people.

On Wednesday Ed, Mila, Eugenia, Caleb, and I went to Starbucks downtown at 5:45 a.m. and had coffee and talked and watched the city come to life. Glorious. It was like I had friends.

This coffee tastes like warm soy milk. I want to more fully realize that my life is beautiful and I can do whatever I want, and be whoever I want, and I don't have to listen to anyone. I can do my own thing. I don't have to follow societal rules and norms. I don't have to conform. I don't have to be a part of anyone's definition of anything.

I am nothing, and because of this I am everything. Because I take a little chunk of everything I see, incorporate it into myself, and become less a part of any one group. It makes sense. I am enamored with this idea. I don't have to go through the appropriate motions. I can fuck up, I can learn from my mistakes, from other people's mistakes. I don't have to follow a plan.

Well, I think I have said all that needs to be said.

10 May 2010

I went to Lillian's house over the weekend. Her family is hilarious! We went to Leavenworth, this little touristy German town in the mountains with a million shops. I bought a Hello Kitty tin case and we all ate ice cream. I also tried this hot sauce, regardless of Lillian's friend Kayla's advice not to, and I almost died. I was drooling for, like, 20 minutes even though I drank a bottle of milk. I ate so much that day.

We also went to Lillian's high school to listen to Kayla sing and play guitar. She's brilliant. Lillian's mom is obsessed with the dollar store, so we went there as well and she let us buy three things. I think she goes there, like, every day, it's the best thing ever. We went to a thrift store and I got a tank top for $1.50. Finally, we went to this Mexican grocery store and her mom spoke Spanish to everyone. Fucking cool.

Today's Monday. I got a lot of sleep and it feels good. I'm at the library downtown, going to check out two more movies. I watched *Paprika* last night and I loved it, although I didn't really understand the whole thing. I couldn't figure out the difference between dreams and reality.

I have pilates tonight with my team. I may or may not run before. I feel like I should, but I also hate when I pressure myself to do things I feel like I should do. I have a lot of shit to do and I want to get it done.

What would the world be like if I didn't have this nuisance of a mind?

16 May 2010

I woke 30 minutes ago. Roommates are gone, everything's calm, Sunday, hot coffee I made in my room. I wanted to feel like I'm at home and it's summer, waking late and drinking coffee while reading on the couch, watching the day unfold till I feel the need to get up and do something.

A whole week has slipped past me, what have I been doing? Friday night we went camping. It was okay, not that many people went. I think most of them went last night. We got drunk and I ate a ton of shit. S'mores with Reese's instead of chocolate!

We slept in Claire's car, who is another freshman on the team. She transferred here from another school so she wasn't here at the beginning of the year. I slept under a couple coats because Brendan ripped his blanket and pillow away from me in the middle of the night. Haha. I stole them because I went to sleep before him and they were in Claire's car, and when he came to get them he saw me and was like, "Aw, hell no!" It was funny but it sucked because then I was freezing for the rest of the night.

Brendan is just some random guy on the men's soccer team. I don't know him that well because he doesn't hang out with the guys on the team that I hang out with. He doesn't seem like that interesting of a person, to be honest.

Last night Kan and I watched *Changeling* in her apartment. Angelina Jolie is such a good actress, I got chills watching her. Today I'm going to go to the street fair in UW. Yesterday I went downtown with Lillian, Al, Jean, another random girl that lives on our floor in the dorms, and two of Lillian's friends that go to UW. It was sunny and nice and there were a million people out. Fabulous! Today looks nice as well, as far as I can tell. I've been trying to live in the moment, and truly enjoy what I'm doing, but time is running too quickly. It's hard to be here now.

Oh, I forgot to say that we took the ferry back to Seattle from where we were camping, and it was beautiful. The view of the city was intense and unjustified by my flimsy fisheye lens.

19 May 2010

Kurt Cobain and Andy Warhol exhibit at the Seattle Art Museum.

24 May 2010

So much to say. Right now I'm in the laundry room waiting for my clothes to dry. It's peaceful. The sound of the dryer is comforting and it's warm in here. I'm alone.

It reminds me of a recurring instance when I was little. I would play in the living room with the sun drifting through the windows, a sun not of the morning or afternoon. A time-less sun. The dishwasher was always on, a low roar representing my mother's responsibility. A safe situation, a place in which I'd still reside if not for time's limitless future.

Sometimes I go to that place before I fall asleep at night. Nostalgia suffocates me and as I die I enter the escapist's realm and everything is perfect.

Anyway, over the weekend I flew back to Idaho for my cousin Maddie's wedding. She was beautiful, and when they kissed it was for a long time, and she grabbed him back when he pulled away.

I hung out with Camila all weekend and whenever I'm at her house I can't stop thinking of all the things we've done together. All the ridiculous inside jokes and adventures. I miss it so much I can't stand it. Growing older is hard.

At the wedding reception Dad got really drunk (as usual haha) and was picking up chairs and waving them around and yelling and dancing. After the reception the party moved to Camila's house in her dad's huge shop. I drove us there and I was secretly drunk, but Dad couldn't drive because he was wasted so I was the runner-up.

Sawyer was pissed because he knew I was drunk and shouldn't be driving. But it was fine. I drank the vodka Sawyer bought me, and I got to see Bob and Joel and Weston and Alex. The usual drunken foolishness and hilarity. I love those people. I never feel bad when I'm around them.

26 May 2010

I keep feeling excited. About summer, about doing my own thing. Not letting people take advantage of me, not letting them make me do things I don't want to do. I'm struggling to find meaning in a chaotic, hostile world. Where people try to change you into what they want you to be.

There's too much corruption in the world, too many people out there that are ready to exploit you. How can I avoid this? How can I not exploit others? It seems like behind every story of success, prosperity, and love, there is a story of terrible meaninglessness and exploitation. This makes me feel uncomfortable and uneasy and scared.

I can't figure out what is right and wrong, or the difference between these. I don't know what I'm doing, what I want to do.

Why do we want things to be meaningful so badly?

Kan: judgmental, critical. She doesn't understand that everyone is different, that no one is like her, exactly. She doesn't understand that I see the world differently, that I respond to things *differently*, not *better* or *worse*, just in my own way. She is really concerned with "better or worse." There is no ultimate right or wrong, better or worse, because everyone has different thresholds for different things. There can be better or worse for an individual on a personal level, but not for the general public.

Kan's competitive, she has to be the best. And she thinks that everyone has to reach her standards for living, which are *very* high. I don't want to hang out with her all the time now because she makes me anxious. She makes me feel like I'm being less of myself, like she's changing me into someone I don't want to be. I hate it.

A lot of the time I feel like I am completely myself only when I am alone. Because everyone, no matter how long I've known her, has opinions and perspectives of me that do not coincide with my intentions or true feelings. Truth and Reality are without feeling or perspective. They just *are*. There's no judgment.

It's hard because you can't please everyone. There will always be someone that has negative opinions of you that you can't change, and it's not your fault. It's nobody's fault. It's just that you are different people from each other and one of you doesn't understand, or both don't understand, that no one can be the same or respond to stimuli the same way.

All of that being said...Kan's still my best friend. Truly. Like, my first *real* best friend that actually understood and *listened.* No one has ever truly listened to me voice my actual, real feelings with such depth and patience.

28 May 2010

Today's Friday. It's 10:24 p.m. I'm alone in my room.

Camila, her boyfriend Bob, and their friend Will came to Seattle today and we all hung out. We went to a tattoo place in Wallingford because Bob wants to get a tattoo tomorrow, so we had to check it out. They are getting drunk with a friend tonight. I didn't want to go with them. I wanted to be alone tonight, and so far it's been relaxing.

I've been listening to music and working on my artistic project for my Core class. Three-day weekend! Then four days of school, weekend, finals, and *home*. Fuckin' fabulous. I'm excited to be alone and do my own thing.

01 June 2010

Everything's flying past me. I'm trying to cradle this moment in my hands, pet it and whisper to it and love it, but somehow I can't manage.

As I mentioned before, Camila, Bob, and Will came over for the weekend, and they're already gone. We stayed at their friend Syler's house in Issaquah, a smaller city in Washington. His father is an entomologist. He has the greatest house ever; it's huge and old and antique, inhabited by spiders, skulls, and dead mice. It was messy and smelled like camping. Camila said it reminded her of Grandma's basement when we were little and I completely agree.

I slept in Syler's bed with him and we made out. The next night we slept in his parents' bed. We all drank the first night and the second night only Syler and I drank. We split a bottle of wine. Merlot. He reminded me of Kurt: the same small stature, the same blonde, greasy hair. We all hung out downtown and went shopping, and went with Bob to the tattoo place. We ate ice cream and made new inside jokes.

I feel sad now that they're gone. We had created this bubble world of intoxication and small smiles and the ability to say anything to friends who won't think you're dumb, but it burst when they left.

Now I'm downtown at the public library trying to write a paper. I was looking at my computer, like, ten minutes ago, and I looked up randomly and this guy with a huge camera was taking my picture. It was weird. I looked back at my screen quickly and pretended I didn't notice. I was the only person in the direction he was pointing his camera so I assume it was me he was photographing.

I kind of like this sad feeling. It's weird how that can happen. One of the things I loved about this weekend was that I felt so real. Like, I wish that was my life. I wish Syler and I had that house to ourselves, or at least that it was mine in some way. I'm yearning for randomness and beauty to be incorporated into my life. I am super sick of this Christian shit, I want to be around normal people. I want to have experiences like this past weekend to be regular occurrences.

I dunno if I want to go here next year, but I have to. I will try it one more time and see what happens. I'm wondering if my negativity is just how I am, if I'll be that way no matter where I am. It's quite possible.

03 June 2010

I was just at the Seattle Art Museum, to see Kurt Cobain one more time. I'm in love with him. I want to be him so badly, to feel what he felt, the pain and the glory, the lust and self-loathing. I don't want to be anyone else.

I wonder if he had ever felt what I feel now, about someone else. Why do I feel this way? Why do I feel like he's somehow better than everyone else? Because he's skinny and dirty? And ugly and intensely attractive at the same time? Because he was depressed and felt things?

It's my mind's creation of his personality that I want to be and experience and love so badly that it hurts my throat and I feel like someone is putting pressure on my entire body. I almost started crying at the exhibit. He's dead, but I want to put my hands on his shoulders and push him up against the wall, press my body against his, put my fingers in his hair, breathe softly into his ears without saying anything.

Yesterday I hung out with Syler on the Ave, since he didn't have to leave with Camila and them, and he lives only, like, 20 minutes away. We played backgammon and drank coffee and got sushi and walked around all the shops. We watched a movie in the lounge in my dorm. It was fun, but...I dunno.

I walked him to his car and tried to kiss him before he left, but it seemed like he didn't want to. We sort of held hands while watching the movie, and I know he likes me or he wouldn't be hanging out with me. So, yeah. I dunno what's happening with that. It feels different now that Camila is gone.

I love grunge. Where are all these people that are in bands? Where do they hang out? I want to be a part of that. I'm not a part of anything.

05 June 2010

I am at a coffee shop with Jean, Lillian, and Natalie. I studied for Design for a bit. I don't have much to do other than that.

Yesterday I saw a movie with Syler downtown. We held hands. He grabbed my hand in the middle of the movie. I dunno why everyone likes holding hands; it's not that cool. I actually don't even like it because your hands end up getting sweaty, and my fingers always get cold.

He dropped me off at my dorm and we made out in his car for the longest time. Like right in front of the dorm. I bet people could see us. It was the greatest thing ever; he is an awesome kisser.

I also went downtown with Tabby (the girl from my Middle Ages class) and Lillian yesterday. Tabby got her ears pierced. It was ridiculous. She is such a baby. She had to get both ears pierced at once because she was scared, and it took forever because she was freaking out the whole time.

I fell asleep in the food court at the mall because I only got, like, four hours of sleep the night before. I had woken up at five in the morning for no reason and I couldn't fall back asleep so I just stayed up.

Lately I have been *obsessed* with Kurt, I don't even know why. I think he's the cutest thing ever. I love his grunge style and his scraggly unwashed hair. I think he is hella sexy. I bet partially the reason why I love him is because of his vulnerability, his sensitivity. I'm pretty sure he was depressed. I love when guys are sensitive and perceptive, and feel things differently than others.

I know I'm definitely creating a personality for him that I'm attracted to, but I don't care. I imagine him as being alone, as being great, as being misunderstood. As being fucking real. As being whatever he wanted without being under a label or stereotype.

I'm attracted to all of these characteristics probably because I wish I could encompass them, probably because I already am a few of them. I wish somebody thought of me in the way I think of him. He is fucking cool. I want to be cool. I want to be important and meaningful. I want to think of myself as cool.

07 June 2010

I'm in the reading room at the public library. Tenth floor.

Today's been warm. I sat in the grass by Pike's, closed my eyes, wondered why I feel Kurt Cobain is better than everyone else. Is it the fame? I know it's not the money. I like dirty, I like grunge. Is it the importance I feel emanates from his memory?

Tonight I'm going to Bauhaus with Kan and Eugenia to study for Anthropology. Actually, it will just be us reading to each other.

I like my look today. I want to buy cigarettes. I painted the tips of my nails red, it looks good.

Yesterday I walked around Fremont with the intent of buying mota brownies and the lady wasn't there, so I went there for nothing. It was lame. I'm renting *Bleach: The Movie* from the library. It's going to be hella sweet.

I haven't worked out in forever, it makes me anxious. Who the fuck cares, though? I'm going to do whatever the fuck I want. I think I'm going to leave the library. I dunno what else to say. Yesterday was lame; I didn't know what to do. Today's been better. I don't know what I'm going to do with my life. It makes me nervous.

09 June 2010

I'm drunk. Was at the sophomore soccer girls' apartments. I

wanted to remember this moment. Ana, please remember this carefree feeling. Love yourself. Like you love Kurt.

Max said he wasn't himself, Calvin said he'd fuck me, didn't understand why guys haven't fucked me. Trevor said he worshipped me. Brendan was creepy. Kan kissed Calvin. I ate and I said I wouldn't. We're all fools. Cameron went to bed early. There weren't that many people there. I wore Eugenia's spandex. I talked to Drake on the roof about the clouds, how they were fast and close. I told him guys are fucked up.

I said goodbye to the Space Needle because I'm going home for the summer. I love that view so much. Natalie's gone, our room's empty, back to normal. It's weird. I think I'm gonna go to bed. I love you. I am you.

10 June 2010

Lillian moved out today so I'm alone in our room right now. I'm basically all packed. I cleaned my desk and dresser. Jean left as well. Today I wanted to go on a run but I never did. Bleh. Kurt Cobain. I took a two-hour nap today because I had a headache and felt super bloated and gross. I don't know what to do with myself. This is strange to me, everything being packed, our room back to normal. I don't know how to react.

12 June 2010

Home for summer. I couldn't relax today because there was this undercurrent of anxiety in my head, I dunno why. I think it was about soccer, about my summer workouts. I haven't received them in the mail yet, but I felt worried about them and couldn't stop thinking about it. Scared, kind of. Because I'm not a real person and I can't just fucking relax. I hate it.

Skip a fucking workout, it doesn't matter. I shouldn't need to exercise every day to keep the anxiety out. I think maybe exercising clears my head, and it's either do that to empty out all the shit, or meditate, and I'm still afraid to meditate. I honestly am terrified of my own mind, and I'm not sure if I am ashamed to say that. I don't want to feel meaningless fear or anxiety, and sometimes I think meditation brings that stuff to the surface of my consciousness, probably because it's hiding out there.

Sometimes I wonder if there is so much pent up worry inside my head that it comes out at random moments, like today. There really was no reason for me to feel uncomfortable. It was only a normal day, relaxing. I didn't do anything important, just rearranged my room a bit, cut pictures out of magazines, watched *Public Enemies* with Dad.

While watching *Public Enemies* I tried to become John Dillinger. I tried to feel what he felt. Because in the movies the characters are glorified in a way, whether they are good or bad. It's like no matter who you are, you'd rather be the person in the movie, because somehow they are important. It is strange to me.

I feel nervous because I am not the people in the movies. I am boring and my existence is insignificant and futile. Why does this make me scared? Why do I feel so bad when I feel unimportant? If I could just feel comfortable with my life and what I'm doing, feel like I am interesting and worth knowing, then I could view myself in the revering mindset I view the people I see as real. And everything would be okay instead of weird and confusing and pointless.

14 June 2010

I've already accomplished a lot and I've only been home for a few days.

Yesterday I went mountain biking with Dad and it was a good workout. I crashed going down because I suck at steering. Today I woke at 5:50 a.m., not on purpose. I set my alarm for 6:30 so I could go give plasma early, but I woke up earlier for some reason.

Anyway, I couldn't give plasma because I have to get a note from the people that pierced my lip saying they did it sterilely. And even if I did do that I wouldn't be able to start giving until July, and I don't think it's worth it to go through all the procedures in order to give for, like, two months. So I think I'm going to get my nose pierced to spite them. Haha. And it's on my list of things I want to do, so yeah.

Oh, also, I started writing a book. With my diaries. All I've done so far is organize thoughts and write down a few entries from the first three diaries I've written. Honestly, I think it's dumb. All my entries sound foolish. Now I'm depressed because I'm imagining looking back on this entry here and thinking, "Wow, what an immature dumbass!" Ugh. Hopefully it'll get more interesting. I want to like it and right now I really don't.

I always think about how many people in the world are trying to write a book and get it published, and I think mine is probably shit compared to others. I dunno. It's probably not going to have a plot either, because I don't want to mention people's names. I dunno, it's weird. I was just reading through past entries in this diary, and they are loads better than the ones I've been reading that came before. So there's still hope.

There was a lightning storm tonight, Dad and I watched. The

sky was dark, almost reddish brown. The flashes were purple. The drops of rain earlier were plump and sounded luscious upon impact with the pavement.

I've been reading a lot lately. *Zen and the Art of Motorcycle Maintenance.* It seriously puts my insanity into coherent speech. In writing. On paper that is real. It's how I know I'm still sane.

It's midnight. I don't want to go to bed. I talked to Syler on Facebook chat today, he's cute. I think I've been realizing that I like Seattle better than here. I like home, but I don't like Boise because it's bland. Seattle is fucking weird and I think I need that.

Oh, on Wednesday I have to go to court for the shoplifting thing. Not excited. Ah well, life goes on, I guess. I'll get through it easily enough.

Today Mom was like, "I thought I was having an asthma attack during the night so I put my pajama bottoms on because I didn't want you guys to find me dead without my pants on."

18 June 2010

I went to court for the shoplifting thing and it was fine. All I have to do is pay a fine, which I already did, do four days of community service, which I already wanted to do at the animal shelter and I think I'll be able to do it there, and take an anti-theft class all day on a Saturday. So it's not that big of a deal, I guess. Just a nuisance.

19 June 2010

I need to say a lot of shit. I'm on the roof of my house. Today is Saturday. I feel super bloated and bleh. We had a BBQ today with basically all of my family from Dad's side, and Lacy. All day I snacked and was bored and didn't want to talk to anyone. I felt bloated and fat and gross all fucking day, it's stupid.

Sawyer and Lacy's relationship is weird to me. I feel like she ties him down, or, like, bosses him around. I feel bad for him, but I guess he likes it or he wouldn't be with her. I feel jealous though, because I want to hang out with him, but I can't because he's always hanging out with her. And I feel like finally I'm old enough to actually be friends with Sawyer and have a real conversation with him, but it's hard when Lacy is always there because she dominates the conversation. I dunno. I feel like I don't really know my own brother, and I'd like to, but I can't because someone else is getting to know him.

Also, I've been realizing how I am not special. Like, some people are just different, gifted, special. Like fucking Einstein or something. Kurt Cobain. People that have real talents and put them to use. I'm not one of those people, so why do I always feel like them? Why do I feel unique sometimes, like I have something that's fucking important?

I was thinking about how I started writing that book, and I feel like it's lame. Like, nobody cares, why would anyone care about the immature thoughts of some depressed high school kid? I dunno if *I* even care. I only think they're interesting because they're *my* thoughts.

I don't want to be another nobody living in Boise fucking Idaho and hating my life, for the entirety of it. I'd rather be a nobody in Seattle or some other big city and build relationships with people that are at least interesting!

Here I am, biting my nails, dreading the future, bored with the present, and half-regretting the past.

20 June 2010

I'm drinking hard lemonade; Sawyer bought me some yesterday.

I feel weird, down kinda. Dreading the workouts for soccer, which start tomorrow. It's dumb, it's not even gonna be hard. All I have to do is go on a 45-minute run. Easy. I'm just nervous about starting all over again, a new school year. I'm nervous because I don't want a repeat of last year. And, I dunno, maybe I'm a little lazy and a little bored. Maybe I don't wanna work so hard, maybe I don't wanna do the same things over again.

I also feel sad kinda, empty. Probably because fucking Kurt Cobain is dead, probably because I hate myself for feeling uncomfortable in situations that I'm not completely familiar with. Like going to people's houses that are kind of dirty, or old looking, like Jenna's. Not old like antique, old like out of style. I dunno, I'm clearly insane.

I'm bored and I keep thinking about the futility of it all. I'm going to be in this house all summer because there's nowhere else to go. I don't even want to hang out with anyone! Or maybe I do, I just become incapacitated when I think about calling someone because phones give me anxiety. I think I'm gonna go write my book, which I think is stupid but I'm not gonna quit. Ugh!

21 June 2010

Today I woke up and made coffee and came out on the porch

to write, which is where I am now. It's calming, everything's quiet. This is an intensely private moment I think. I'm entirely myself. Mornings are my favorite. Quiet, coffee, warm, plump with opportunity.

I like Kurt because he has taught me something. He has shown me that it's okay to be poor, it's okay to sleep in a box on your friend's porch, it's okay to feel like shit. Because that's life and it's fucked up, and it's beautiful because it's fucked up. It shouldn't make you feel uneasy. He failed so many fucking times before Nirvana made it big, so I don't need to worry about anything. He lived in dirty places. It's okay, that's real. I don't need everything to be perfect.

Also, I was thinking that even if I'm typing out all my diary entries for nothing, I don't care because it's interesting to go through them and remember. There are also things I've written down that are important and need to be remembered, just for the sake of…my mental health, I guess. So it's okay. I just hate doing things for nothing, but I think that's something I need to get over because it's part of life.

I think a lot of the time I shield myself from life, like emotional parts of life that happen to everyone. I think I have a lot of pride, and I don't want to feel hurt by anything because that would injure my pride, so I shield myself from it. I distance myself from others because it's too scary to open up to them. I think I'm scared of a lot of stuff.

I can't figure out if I'm afraid to fail, or if I'm afraid of shattering people's expectations of me, or if I hate when people expect good things from me because I hate myself. Maybe I am afraid of doing well and fulfilling their expectations, because I hate that they have those expectations. But, I don't see why I would be afraid of doing well.

That reminds me of that one quote I see everywhere, I dunno it word for word or who even said it, but it's basically saying that we aren't afraid of failing, we are afraid of accomplishing everything we're capable of. But that doesn't make any sense to me. Why the fuck would I be afraid of that? Because it sounds pretty nice to me. Maybe that is my pride talking and I don't want to give up my negativity because it's mine and it's special, and it spawns creativity. And it'll be gone if I succeed so completely.

Maybe I'm afraid of succeeding to my full capacity because it doesn't end there. You have to keep it up, it isn't static. You have to keep working hard and evolving and becoming better, and I'm a lazy person.* It's much easier for me to wallow in my own self-doubt than accomplish something. Hmm. No. No, I'm afraid of working hard, not succeeding. Succeeding naturally follows (or it should) from hard work, and I'm inherently lazy. That makes much more sense! Why would I be afraid of success if it wasn't hard? I wouldn't be.

[*Ana: You're not lazy, you just don't like doing things that you don't want to do. –J.]

22 June 2010

Last night I was writing my book and then randomly didn't feel like it anymore, so I closed my computer and turned on the TV, and I found a documentary on Courtney Love on VH1. And it was just starting to get into her relationship with Kurt, and I was like, "What the fuck!" It was like fate! I mean seriously, why would I turn to that channel at that precise moment? It's crazy, right when I'm obsessed with Nirvana, that happens. So weird. It was like something that only happens in the movies. Ha. Maybe I'm being a bit dramatic. But I've really started liking Courtney Love, too.

Anyway, today I have to go to the jail and figure out my community service shit, and then I'm going to do my workout.

23 June 2010

Please make a statement about me. Tell me something I'm overlooking. Tell me who I am.* Why do I have to say everything I've done? Why does pen on paper feel luxurious? Why am I so fucking precise? This is abnormal. FUCK OFF.

I'll be very precise in exploring the question of why I'm precise. More background info means more understanding of what I feel at that moment? And I wanna see what I did when this is long forgotten. See? Easy. That wasn't too hard.

Why am I obsessed with celebrity? Why do I think the only people that are important are famous?

[*Ana: You're Saturn disguised as Venus. You're big Capricorn energy. You're everything about the 12th house. –J.]

24 June 2010

Yesterday I hung out with Davis at a coffee shop. We played backgammon and cards. I obliterated him. I also downloaded Courtney Love's band, Hole, which is what I'm listening to right now. I like the songs "Celebrity Skin" and "Malibu." I decided Courtney Love is the shit! She has such a great voice. It reminds me of Kim Gordon when she, like, croons, and then when she yells it's all raspy and kickass.

26 June 2010

Two days ago I went on a run and when I got back home I

saw this glowing orb thing on the front patio. I felt dizzy and weird, so I called Dad and fell into bed, and apparently I had a seizure. My brain was swollen or something. Dad drove really fast to the hospital and was honking at everyone and being super worried.

Because of that Mom and I couldn't go to Lewiston, which we were planning, because I am supposed to stay close to a hospital in case it happens again. Then I slept for a long time.

Today Sawyer and I bzzzed at a coffee shop. I finished reading *Zen and the Art of Motorcycle Maintenance*, and I started a new book called *Eat When You Feel Sad*. I think I'm going to go to bed.

I'm pissed I couldn't go to Lewiston. They're having a party tonight. Without me. And Syler is there and I'm totally in love with him.

I brushed my teeth and then had a midnight snack, but I refuse to brush them again. I'm kind of pissed right now. I'm ugly, fat. I hate myself and I want to die.

28 June 2010

I think I can write things that make people feel things. Sometimes.

30 June 2010

The day before yesterday I hung out with Eli. We hung out by his pool and then drank his parents' alcohol because they're on vacation somewhere. His brother and sister were gone, too.

Dad put road tires on my bike! I'm excited, I'm going to ride my bike around Gasworks, like, every day. I decided that I'm going to get a job in downtown Seattle if it's the last thing I do. I want to so badly, it feels super real to me. I would feel like such a real person if I got a job downtown. I could ride the bus or ride my bike.

What if Sawyer and I got an apartment together? I really want that to happen. Then I wouldn't have to live with annoying Christians, and we could do cool shit. And we'd both have Seattle jobs and get out of Boise and love life. I always invent situations like this. It's the best thing ever because it makes me excited about life and existing, even if it might not (or probably won't) happen.

01 July 2010

I was texting Kan about my seizure, and I told her that it was a good excuse to not do the workouts. I said that I thought they were stupid anyway, and that they stressed me out and I didn't even care, and that I was just going to run every day and not worry about doing the exact planned workout. She was like, "Why don't you care?" And I realized, in that moment, that she doesn't understand me at all.

Maybe I am terrible at communicating how I feel, but I dunno. I don't always think that's it. I am the type of person that likes to do my own thing and not follow any type of schedule. If I am forced to follow a set schedule with certain activities that must be completed a certain way, I get too anxious and I can't do my best. I need to do things at my own pace and how I want to do them.

I was thinking about playing soccer for my club team before college, and how I was really good, and why that was. I'm pretty sure it was because I was allowed the freedom to do whatever I wanted. I could eat whatever I wanted before practice or games, and at whatever time I wanted, rather than four hours before, like it is now.

Also, as a center mid I was permitted to go all over the field; I didn't have to follow stupid rules about defending, about when to step and when to stay. I wasn't required to follow the other team's center mid around. Rather, it was better that I got away from her so that I could get the ball from my own team. I was allowed to focus on myself and playing well, rather than worrying about what other people were doing.

So I'm going to try to do my own thing from now on. I'm not going to worry about the workouts. I'll still run and stuff, but I'm not going to get anxious about changing the workouts, which includes not doing certain activities that are outlined in the packet.

I'm not going to let Kan stress me out, because she's too fucking good at that, and I hate it. I'm going to do whatever I want. Now that I know everyone on the team and am comfortable with them, it'll be fine and dandy. It's hard for me to not let Kan make me feel bad about myself. It's the weirdest thing. She's just kind of self-righteous and acts like she's the best at everything, and it makes me feel shitty. Like, she acts like she's better than me at everything. I dunno. She psychs me out. It sucks. Well, fuck her. Who cares what she's doing? I'm going to do my own thing and worry about myself.

Also, another reason why I can't do strict schedules is because it makes me feel like I'm not a real person. Like I'm a slave, kind of. I don't have freedom, and that's frustrating.

When I think about it, I think Eli really gets me. Like, he has the same kind of mindset as me. He wants to play soccer, but that isn't the only thing he is. He wants to be a real person and do other things as well. He doesn't like being tied down by soccer. He says it is like they "own" you and dictate everything you do. I think it's definitely true, but only in college.

Club soccer and high school soccer was such a good way to release positive, genuine energy, *your* energy: *you*. In college, or university, your soul is sucked out. Chadwick will zap every bit of positive energy you have left by requiring you to do every little thing the way he wants it to be done. And if you don't do it his way, you get in trouble and have to have a meeting where he interrogates you about your actions. Say goodbye to any wavelength of free energy flowing creatively. Ciao.

04 July 2010

This weekend we went to Ketchum, where Sawyer currently works, to go camping with him and Lacy. Today we went hiking and yesterday we went on a bike ride to downtown Ketchum and Sun Valley. There were tons of people since it's a holiday weekend.

There's this long path for runners and bikers that we rode on that goes for a few miles, and it was beautiful out! Bright sun in a sky with blocky clouds, hot but breezy. My sunglasses make everything look deeply saturated: a bursting, rich vibrancy. I took a lot of pictures with my fisheye camera.

Riding my bike in the sun and the breeze, I looked up when I passed under these trees with white flowers. The clouds above were pure white, the sky penetratingly blue. The contrast between water and atmosphere was linked by this brilliant, shining sun. It was how you'd expect to feel upon meeting a god you've had faith in for your entire life.

I thought about how I was in that moment, and the glory of what was outside my mind and how I could perceive it. I thought about how I always have that mind, and how I should be able to recreate that sense of awe and joy in any moment. I will use that moment in my mind as a place of safety to go to when things are bad.

I am always who I am regardless of my surroundings. Is this not true? One can never be sure.

A lot of the time I imagine that your situation should be irrelevant when determining your mood. I might as well still be there right now, as I sit at the bar in the kitchen of the home I grew up in. Alone and still, quiet but for the ticking of the clock and the distant bombs of Independence Day, a pen in hand, writing under the light of the single bulb above the stove.

I remember the feeling of yesterday. I caress its silky skin with the neurons in my brain. I can be that moment now, again. I can be that moment over and over, forever.

Even this moment, here, is beautiful. I will hold it in the dark behind my eyelids, to be revisited a million times a day. Tomorrow, when there is labor to be toiled over, I can use this machine upon my shoulders to feel what I want to feel, to be here now, become yesterday in all its splendor, experience what it's like to be a moment in time.

Tomorrow I have to do the community service thing for my delinquency. It's actually called SILD - Sheriff Inmate Labor Detail. Yay, it's going to be fan-fucking-tastic. Not.

Oh, the funniest thing! My phone died over the weekend, and when I turned it on today while charging it I saw that Syler had texted me at three in the morning saying, "I can't get ahold of you but you're hot." Haha! Seriously made my entire day. Then today he texted me saying, "Sorry that was very forward, I was pretty smashed last night." I thought it was hilarious, he is so cute.

05 July 2010

SILD was okay. I got to go to this bird rehabilitation place and it was actually a neat experience. I got to hand feed the birds in the aviaries, and I did a lot of cleaning - washing dishes, sweeping one of the aviaries, odd jobs.

For lunch we were given bologna sandwiches. I only ate the bread because the meat had been sitting out in these coolers since 7 a.m., and they didn't have ice or anything in them. Gross! It was shitty. All in all though, I'm kind of glad I did it because I had been wanting to volunteer at a place like that anyway, so whatever. I was a bit dehydrated at the end because when my mom picked me up I felt sick. But she bought me an ice cream cone and it made me feel a lot better.

Right now I'm listening to Spoon in my room. Davis just called me and invited me to go to the hot springs with him tomorrow. Nooo! I'm going to make up some excuse not to go.

06 July 2010

Today's been…okay. I dunno. I keep getting these tiny glimpses of worry about soccer. I think it's because I'm not that excited about it. Like, I'm kinda dreading it because it's going to be hard. Well, not that it's hard, but that it takes up so much time and I can't do my own thing or be my own person. Like living in the apartments. I wanna buy food that is good and try to take my time when getting good deals, but my teammates just rush through it and it makes me crazy because I'm anal about money and we have to share it to buy food.

I've also been dreading the rest of my SILD stuff. After feeling sick after the first one I'll probably feel awful and faint or something if I have to do something worse, like walking on the freeway picking up trash. Ugh. I'm not looking forward to this.

Anyway, nothing that cool has happened today. I rented seven movies from the library. Tonight I'm going to watch *A Scanner Darkly*. Keanu Reeves. Sex.

07 July 2010

I've been thinking about this a lot lately: everything is better in Seattle than in Idaho. Or anywhere else is better than Idaho, for that matter. I cannot figure out why I think this. If two identical items were in Boise and Seattle, I would automatically classify the Seattle one as better. I am crazy.

And right now I am so bored. And annoyed at all the shit I have to do, like appointments and all this stuff that restricts my schedule. I think I start to get irritable and bored and depressed when I'm at home all day, because nothing ever happens and I hate being in Boise and I feel like I'm going insane. I don't want to spend any money because I have to pay for my delinquency, and I can't drive or do anything alone because I might have a seizure, which I know I will probably never have again. Ugh. Kill me.

10 July 2010

This isn't important unless I'm famous, or I die suddenly and tragically, or I have a huge impact on someone. It's all perspective! If someone who thought I was brilliant in some way discovered this diary, maybe they'd think it was real and artistic. If someone that didn't give a shit about me found it they'd probably discard it the same way I disregard people in conversations because I'm standoffish. What else do I need to say?

I've been writing my book and I think it's shit. I hate it. Everything I've said is stupid and irritating and immature. Normally this iconoclastic behavior would be interesting, but only if it's someone else's. Only if it is of someone I find intriguing. No one gives a shit because I'm not famous. I don't know anything about life and I don't want to deal with people criticizing me for things I hate about myself. God, it's just circles and circles. I want to be influential. I love that I hate myself, and the other way around. I can never say what's in my mind, no one can understand!

Last night Lacy, Sawyer, and I went to these sand dunes to stargaze for Lacy's astronomy class, and it was pure. Billions of stars, the Milky Way, so startlingly visible. Rapture. We climbed a small dune and I covered myself in sand, and I was every single star. I swear I was. I was every galaxy in that sublime night sky.

It's fucking mind-blowing how everything is so much bigger than my puny existence. How can I care about anything when it's clearly irrelevant? How can I worry about running every day for soccer when there could be people like me on other planets, alone and hypnotized by the blackness of the cosmos, feeling the same helplessness and confusion apparent in my own tiny mind? This is the most significant thing in the universe.

We drank alcohol. I don't know if there's anything else worth mentioning right now.

15 July 2010

In Lewiston! Haven't written in a while. I've been too preoc-
cupied with Grandma and Camila. It's been lovely. Oh, um…
Camila and I kind of got tattoos. On our butts. Of our secret
password from our childhood. Ha! The guy that did them was
wearing a kickass Gorillaz shirt, and there was a drawing of
Kurt Cobain on the wall that he had done, so basically it was
meant to be.

19 July 2010

Today I had my third day of SILD, which wasn't bad at all!
We planted flowers all day, real relaxing. One more day, next
Monday. Dad and I also saw *Inception*, it's this new movie
about dreams with Leo DiCaprio. Quality.

Right now I'm lying on my floor listening to music. Candles
lit. My room is safe. It's messy and lived in. Clothes strewn
across the floor, dim lights. I'm alone, sheltered by the
crowded vibrating pulse of familiarity. The items revolving
around my mind create soft rhythms that flow through me,
letting memories and secrets of the past seep into my pores.

I know a hidden history of a self that may or may not exist. I
am here, now, and this is the most significant situation in my
life, soon to be forgotten among dreams and to-do lists,
appointments and calls from friends. I'll disregard this
moment until a future chance encounter with this simple diary
entry. One minute point in a lifetime of tiny yet endless
occurrences. Everything is in the right place. Random, unor-
ganized, perfect, impermanent.

Yesterday we drove to the ski hill about an hour away from
the city so Dad could mountain bike and I could run. It was

colder up there, and completely quiet but for the birds. Solitude. My run was mostly downhill, and now my quads scream with the remembrance of strange muscles becoming active.

Oh, I started reading the book *Dune*. It's cool.

20 July 2010

I'm so bored I could die. I hate the sun, the ice cream man, Boise, running, not running, being bored when nothing sounds good to do. I don't want to do anything. I'm on the front porch, slight breeze, cooler now since it's the beginning of the evening.

Gene, our family friend since forever, died but I don't really feel anything.

Tomorrow is my MRI to see if anything is wrong with me that made me have a seizure. I'm irritated and frustrated and bored and pissed.

Fuck zen, fuck meditation. I'm going to live a shit life and I'm going to be happy about it. I hate living here, I have no friends, no one understands. I'm not famous. I'm someone you don't know and have never heard of. These are my secrets.

I'm a junkie. I get my fix when pen meets paper. I have nothing to say but I've got to keep going or I'll start feeling bad again. I'm dependent upon this process that purges. Does it actually purge? Or does it generate more? I'll never know; it hides behind illusion and expectation. I go back to you, again and again, because you're my only one. I truly feel this way, I'm not making this up.

There are more people in the world than your mind can

comprehend. Isn't that the source of all your despair? The stem of all your problems? How can it not be? It created fairness, society, right and wrong, morals, humanity. Damn it all! I don't want anything to do with it.

22 July 2010

I'm nervous because Lisbet and I are supposed to hang out and I haven't seen her in forever. I feel like it could be super awkward and I don't want it to be. I also hate sitting in my house not using the air-conditioning, and being anxious about not doing the soccer workouts perfectly.

Syler Facebook chatted me last night. I love.

27 July 2010

I am done with SILD as of yesterday. Yesterday I saw *Salt* with my dad. He said he liked it better than *Inception.*

Lisbet and I hung out and it was totally fine. I played in her coed soccer game, it was fun. I slept over at her house and we drank wine and smoked mota. And talked.

Mom and I went to the zoo on Sunday.* My favorite animals were the bats. They were huge and looked like miniature upside-down cats. Also, there was this one teeny monkey that liked the ring I was wearing. I kept moving it around in front of the glass and he would follow it and try to smell it. Adorable.

On Saturday we went to the farmer's market. I love being downtown, it's the only interesting thing in Boise. Everything else is shit.

Today we went to my neurologist appointment and my brain

is normal. MRI and EEG were normal. But I'm still not allowed to drive. So I'm going to kill myself instead. I am so fucking I don't know! I hate doing nothing, but when I think of something to do I don't feel like doing it at all. I don't feel like doing anything. I'm just so tired. The heat makes it worse.

I'm supposed to go play soccer with Jessi at eight. She was on the varsity team with Lisbet and I in high school. I think Lisbet's going to come too, not sure. It's making me anxious. Tomorrow Jenna wants to hang out in the morning, which is making me weird because I wanna be alone kinda. Fuck, I'm so anxious!

Mom's always organizing everything, it makes me insane. She's always cleaning and I wish she'd let things not be spotless sometimes.

[*Ana: Zoos are jails for animals. Would you like to be cooped up and stared at for the rest of your life? If not, then why is it okay for other beings to have to live like that? –J.]

28 July 2010

I just got done watching *500 Days of Summer*. I love that movie, probably because the girl reminds me of myself. It's basically a more mature version of what I did to Eli freshman year of high school. I mean, not on purpose, but I didn't like him anymore and didn't know how to tell him. And the guy in it is sexy so it's fun to watch. Haha.

I adore guys like that, that are sensitive and real and genuine. Who like good music and don't want to only get hammered and fuck. I love his personality in that movie. How come there are no guys like that? It makes no sense to me.

Today I did random shit, as usual. But I got stuff done that I wanted to do, like read *Dune* and write my book and sew an orange tank top so that it fits better. Also, I bought table legs from a hardware store and stained them a darker brown, and Dad's going to help me attach them to this vintage suitcase I have that Camila gave me. It's a DIY idea I got from a magazine. I think it'll turn out nice.

29 July 2010

Today I rode my bike to this coffee shop and got an iced tea and worked on my book. I also played in another coed soccer game, and this kid who was on Eli's club team was on my team, and I secretly find him attractive. Actually, he's shorter than me so not really. I just like his face a lot. And he kept telling me good job. So basically he wants me. Haha, just kidding.

I feel like this summer has been a huge waste. I didn't make any money, I didn't go anywhere, I hated myself most of the time. It's depressing. I mean, I did get a lot done I guess, but I dunno. I've been not knowing what to do with myself and being bored and pissed off because of it.

I'm excited to go back to Seattle, but not excited for the soccer part. Which is basically the whole part. Ugh. I want to get a job and an apartment in Seattle. I think that would be fucking neat and I really want it to happen. I guess that's what I'm excited for. I dunno.

30 July 2010

I'm drunk. Ish. I like writing when intoxicated, it's liberating.

We floated the river today and got drunk. Sawyer, Lacy,

Lacy's Indian friend Harsh from college, Lisbet, and me. Lisbet and I had the shittiest raft, so we tried to steal Harsh's raft when we all got out of the water to jump off this huge rock. He was chasing us in the water, and it was scary and funny. It was more fun than I thought it would be, but it felt like it took forever. I got a tad sunburnt.

I'm listening to "Autumn Sweater" by Yo La Tengo. Brilliant. I played soccer with Jessi and Lisbet this morning. We ended up playing world cup with the boys team at our high school. Ridiculous, they are little bastards.

I am not that drunk anymore but I feel good still. I feel excited to do whatever I'm going to do. I am thinking about watching *The Motorcycle Diaries* tonight on my laptop. I've never seen it.

01 August 2010

I've been reading *Persepolis*, the graphic novel. It makes me feel reassured about life. So much shit happened to Marjane, and I love that she just went with it. Maybe she was like me in reality, but in the book she doesn't seem to be anxious. I like her personality a lot and I wish I could be like her. Like…adaptable. I'm unsure how to say what I want to say. It's all in my head but I can't find the right words.

Sawyer's mad at me for putting those table legs on his suitcase, which wasn't even his suitcase. Camila gave it to me forever ago. I'm pretty sure she got it from Grandma, who owned it probably before any of us were even born. He's genuinely pissed at me and giving me the silent treatment. It's making me weird and anxious and I feel like he is being a fucking asshole. Oh well, he'll get over it. We bought him a new one at the thrift store yesterday too, so he should stop being a little bitch.

03 August 2010

I am at a bookstore waiting for my computer to charge so I can write my book. Mom and I got coffee and a small lunch, but she had to go back to work so I'm alone. Less than two weeks before I go back to Seattle.

There are so many books here it's almost threatening. More information than my brain could ever hope to contain, all hovering around me, mocking my lack of time, sneering with creative impunity, passive with a loud brilliance. Do the others see it, too?

04 August 2010

I am hostility.

05 August 2010

We went to First Thursday downtown tonight, it was lovely. All the shops are open late because it's the first Thursday of the month.

I think people watching is one of my favorite things. Dressing up and going places is also one of my favorite activities. "See and be seen." I feel rebellious when I wear crazy clothes, because it's like I'm stating to the public that I'll do whatever the fuck I want, and I don't give a shit about what anyone thinks, which I think is mostly true. So yeah, that's basically all today was good for.

Mom and I are going to Lewiston tomorrow.

09 August 2010

Lewiston was good. Camila and I went to one of her friend's houses because it was their roommate's birthday, and we got drunk. I made out with Weston.

We also dropped Camila off at the university she goes to in Moscow, which is to the north of Lewiston. The university is, like, the main thing in the city. We went to the Saturday market there. A neat experience, great for acquiring creative ideas.

Yesterday we drove back to Boise, it wasn't bad. I slept a lot. When we got back it was hot. I took a nap. I listened to Spoon. The wind started blowing hard, the sky hazy. When the sky gets like that, unsettled, it is as if adventures are brewing around me. I am in the middle of pure change, this dull land is metamorphosing into opportunity and excitement. Interesting.

This morning was hazy too, cool air because the sun was forced into exile. I drank hot coffee on the back porch, a rare occurrence because of the usual heat. Everything felt right. I knew today was going to be all right. Productive yet relaxing. Both my parents came home for lunch so Mom decided it would be cool to drive me to a coffee shop, which is where I reside now. Air-conditioning and no one but me. It's weird to be in an empty coffee shop.

Well, I'm going to write my book now. Today's okay. It's my last week here, then Seattle.

10 August 2010

Ana muses on her sanity in a self-absorbed manner. I can't sleep because I feel too excited. I dunno why. Here is a list of potential candidates: packing, finding a job in Seattle, living in Seattle, saying fuck you to Chadwick if I don't make the fitness tests in the correct time, writing my book, smoking mota and drinking alcohol during season because my future roommate isn't on the team, publishing a book. That is all. I asked Zara before school got out for summer to be my roommate for sophomore year, and she said yes! We are going to live in the same dorm and get crunk all the time.

12 August 2010

Hiya. Today I finished reading *Dune*. It was well written. I actually enjoyed it despite its length and tiny-ass font. I also finished typing out the second part of my book. Now I should edit it. I might take a break, though, until I get settled in Seattle. Not sure. I'm going to read *1984* next. My brain has processed way too much info today.

14 August 2010

I am finally in Seattle, in my parents' hotel. It's hot, no clouds. Strange. We spent today downtown. I showed Mom and Dad all the places I hang out.

For some reason I felt melancholy, like it was a place dear to me, home, that I'd soon never see again. Maybe it's just seeing it again that made me ache with happiness. Maybe I was sad knowing my parents are soon to depart. Maybe I yearn to live downtown and know every person there intimately, to be the spirit of the city when it's dark and secret and quiet in that blaring way. I feel as if I'm missing something vital right as it's encompassing me. It's hidden from me as I stare into its eyes.

We started driving on Friday and stayed the night in Pendleton, Oregon. Our hotel tonight is a dive by the airport. I think it's kickass, it's like an apartment. Mom doesn't think it's that cool, I guess because it's kind of ghetto-ish. We rode the light rail from the airport to downtown. I think I'm going to start taking it when I have to go to the airport instead of getting people to drive me.

Tomorrow I will be reunited with my teammates. I'm excited, I suppose. I think I am more excited to continue my love affair with the city that makes me feel alive. I don't know if I love a human being as much as I love the apartment buildings of old brick, the flowery balconies, the sun glinting on the water, shattering it into a million pieces, representing all that I've cherished and forgotten.

Will I kiss a man as passionately as I've welcomed the shadowy mist into my lungs? As tenderly as I've caressed dirty doorknobs and crept along decrepit back alleys, trash-covered streets and filthy bus seats? Is it possible to long for the moments when I'm alone and goalless, obsessed with achieving nothing, a sojourner of slick sidewalks, letting the rain wash away all that I've cared about and all that I've ever been? Can I honestly say that I will one day love a single person more than I love the raw humanity of all the homeless and crazy and strange combined?

I belong here, in the throbbing heartbeats of the crowded streets, among honks and sirens and screams, hidden behind locked doors and the smell of fish in the coldness. My skin will pale beneath the grayness of the atmosphere as droplets lick my face. People talk to me in the library, bare apartment walls, solitude as the wind bites you, longing to live in those brick buildings because somehow that'd make life worth-while, orange soda in fat bottles,

my miniature error of an existence, never wanting to leave,

cherishing the unproductive wandering of just another evening, squinting when the sun comes out because your eyes aren't accustomed to brightness, coffee from an overrated mega-monster, vibrant colors of edible surprises, lies, the passage of time in its terrifying speed, waves of emotion upon arriving where you want to be.

Pretending you are the people that live in the jungles on the tops of the skyscrapers, worshipping the city and fearing it, wanting to become it more than you've ever wanted anything, and horrified at the thought of this dream coming true. Embracing your own insanity brought on by the loneliness of the streetlights and stop signs in the rain and anticipating when it's legal to walk on the crosswalk.

This moment. This moment. Now, now, now, now. It's slipping by, it's already gone, yet you'll live billions more. Will you waste them? Will you forget them all in the deep waters of your mind? Will your consciousness scatter them, like the light from the sun disturbs the ocean's complacency? How can I know these feelings are true? How can I know they are feelings?

19 August 2010

Thursday. Been here for four days. Two practices a day. Ugh. I made both fitness tests. Mariah and Kan are my roommates in the preseason apartments. Kan has a 23-year-old boyfriend, but he looks like he's 30. He's fat, too.

I hung out with Syler today at a coffee shop. It was fun. I rode my bike there. I'm studying our corner kicks and free kicks, because Chadwick will undoubtedly pick on me, quiz me about technicalities in front of everybody, as he's been doing lately. It makes me feel like an idiot.

I hung out with the junior soccer guys tonight. I like hanging out with them alone because I can be vulgar and impolite and unladylike.

I have not been a real person. I am only a soccer player. It's depressing and all right. I think I should go to a coffee shop tomorrow by myself and write and cry and read and edit my book and be real.

20 August 2010

I'm exactly where I want to be. At a coffee shop again, alone. I only have an hour because they close at nine. I rode my bike here.

This is what life should look like, doing what I want. It's weird how I know that I am pleased when I am in a place I want to be, because either way I'm the same person, wherever I am. At least I feel like I should be the same. How do I know that this is where I want to be?

Practice was okay, Chadwick didn't ask me any questions. Two-a-days are the worst because I can never be alone. I can never be real and feel things; I don't have time. I think I will always be negative about my situation and my circumstances.

I am okay here because I have friends, but sometimes I still doubt myself because I'm not free in the midfield. I am supposed to be doing a certain thing, watching a particular zone. I don't want to, a lot of the time. I'm thinking I won't start. But it shouldn't matter.

We have a scrimmage against ourselves tomorrow. I bet you anything Chadwick will divide us into a team of starters and a team of non-starters, and I'll be on the latter. And for some reason this makes me feel so bad about myself, like I'm worthless. It's stupid.

Everyone is what society has shaped them to be. They're all so trapped by right and wrong, by good and bad. No one can see through it all, see how it's all bullshit. Why can't I find someone who knows these things? Why can't anyone see it?! It's making me insane.

23 August 2010

We had a game and won 2-1. I played okay.

I'm drinking coffee in a teacup and listening to Nirvana. Kan's in the shower, Mariah's in the other room. I put a lamp on the table and this vibe is pleasant and relaxing. Lately we've been crafting in our apartment, it's nice. I've been putting magazine clippings and quotes in my quote/inspiration book.

Yesterday I hung out at the guys' apartments. Boring. Nothing else to say.

25 August 2010

We are all bad people. When you're young you do terrible things, and then you have kids and try to hide from them the terrible things you did. Sometimes you still do them. We all think about creepy, morbid shit, how could you not? There is no right and wrong. There are no windows in this room. I am in a box and I don't know where to go.

Soccer's making me anxious. I feel like I always do the wrong thing, even when I kind of know what I'm doing. It's weird. Sometimes I do the stupidest shit and I have no idea why. Like, I played left back in our last game and I dribbled it straight into the other team twice. I don't know why I did that! Maybe because I'm not a left back? Why did Chadwick put me at left back?

Also, Kan's critical, you really can't be good at anything in her eyes. It's depressing, she makes me feel bad about myself. And she's super narcissistic. She talks about how good she is at everything. It makes me crazy. It makes me doubt myself and play bad. She doesn't understand how my mind works, and she disagrees with me on everything because of this.* She's so fucking hard to live with. I can't wait to move into the dorms with Zara.

Hating yourself spawns creativity, but it's not particularly convenient.

I feel like there's something I'm supposed to be doing right now, and I don't know what it is.

I was thinking that I should be glad it isn't worse. Because it could be way worse. And even if I consider this a failure, it's beautiful, because I finally failed at something. I've talked about how I've wanted to fail before. So I should be glad.

[*Ana: Maybe *you* don't understand how *her* mind works. Either way, it sucks having to adjust yourself to other people's behaviors and psychology instead of living out your own behaviors and psychology in peace.

You should learn the language of astrology already. It's illuminating, it will explain everything. It will help you understand other people and their complicated psychology. You'll see personalities written clearly in symbols and archetypes. You'll see relationships and contradictions between these symbols and archetypes. You'll understand yourself and others much more intensely than ever before. The learning

curve is high, but once you get there, you'll see how everything is connected. –J.]

29 August 2010

Yesterday we played a game in Canada and it was all right. I
played okay, I guess. We tied and Chadwick wasn't happy.

Last night Drake, Max, Ronan, and Trevor came over and
harassed me when I got out of the shower and were saying
that they saw me naked, but they totally didn't. They had
initiations for the freshman and were real drunk. Actually, I
don't think they were that drunk. Anyway, they're dumb.

I wish I didn't have to do anything today. It would be relaxing
and nice. I'm alone right now because everyone's at church.

I woke up alone and looked up out the window at the trees. The
dark green movements. The gray sky that holds all my feelings.
I put my head under the covers and curled up into a little ball
and tried to be a single moment in time. I felt the darkness and
my own body heat. I held inside my mind the fact that under
those covers, isolated and comfortable and hidden, is where
I've wanted to be at so many times in my life.* I'm unable to
bring all those moments into my consciousness because my
brain is too small. I can't fully understand how important that
is, to be able to do that at this time. To be hidden and isolated.
It's all I've ever wanted, can I not cherish it to a full extent?

I also thought about all the places I know exist. I thought
about how right now, at this fleeting second, those places
exist and some are probably inhabited by sentient beings with
their own thoughts and secrets and memories and pain, and
that I'll never know who they are as much as they know
themselves.

158

Grandma's basement growing up, the bathroom in Grandma's new house, my room at home, downtown Seattle, downtown Boise, the Starbucks at Westlake, the bus stop at 3rd and Pine, the coffee shop by my house, the grocery store by my house, the soccer field in Lewiston. Some of these places are inhabited by beings living mundane lives, going through the motions, keeping themselves happy with things that don't matter.

I've been to so many tiny places. Even in one day I can go everywhere. At the end of the day I am everywhere at once because I remember those places and I put them in a small box in my memory. The box is heart-shaped.

[*Ana: You are the definition of the 12th house. –J.]

30 August 2010

Today practice was all right, but I was fucking tired. I just can't make myself run, it doesn't work.

We went to a bonfire with the guys at Golden Gardens. It was fun. I like riding in Claire's car with everyone and listening to the music super loud, even if I don't really like that type of music. It makes me feel like I have friends, like I am having the fun that I always see other people having in pictures on Facebook.

At the same time I see how it's not that cool. I could just as well be alone reading and have as much fun. I'm the same person. I dunno. It's an interesting thought, thought process.

01 September 2010

I feel like everyone on the team thinks I suck at soccer. I

don't know why I feel like I have to be the best at something in order to be valuable as a person.

I feel bad because I realized that I don't care anymore, about soccer, about winning a national championship. I want to care, but I don't. The only thing I care about is avoiding Chadwick's interrogations about why I'm not doing something perfectly, and not being exhausted. Oh, and not making a fool of myself, I suppose.

Every time I get the ball when we're scrimmaging or something, I fuck it up. Give it away, make a bad pass. It's making me insane, because I don't understand why I do it. I think I'm capable of playing soccer on this team, but every time I get the ball my feet don't do what my mind tells them to do. It's so irritating! I can't figure it out.

I'm glad I'm not living in this apartment with Kan and Mariah for the whole year. They are fucking dirty.

Now I'm at Gasworks. It's breezy, sunny, beautiful. More than I could ask for. I wish I could produce long poetic strokes to reveal everything this view makes me feel. In my heart there's a longing to sit here forever and utilize only the five senses, banish thoughts and psychological sensations. No worries, no fears, no anxiety. Calm. The huge, rushing pressure of an atmosphere captured by gravity.

It's insane to me to understand that I'm a human being. I have choices, I have senses. I have this flimsy notebook with the paper fluttering because of the breeze. The warmth on my arm and face. The sting of a cut on my finger, the blood remaining on my pants. My short attention span when trying to write because the view is too breathtaking to be able to concentrate for longer than 30 seconds.

The people I see I will never know, and they have lived whole lives before my eyes have ever acknowledged their existence. Is everyone like me? Does everyone have those secret desires and daydreams and doubts? Does everyone imagine that somehow she is more important than the rest? That she has something special and significant? What if she doesn't have anything special, what then? Does she still have the right to be treated well and with respect?

The poems I wish I could write, the things I'll never say, the things I'll never know or even think of.

One of these days I swear I'm just going to leave and never come back.

author's note

29 July 2020

don't stop digging, magic is the manipulation of energy, who is the lord of your nativity? you are the silence between thoughts, the emptiness of dreamless sleep, the wannabe Underworld Explorer. your fantasy is your mind's coupling with energy frequencies you cannot see or hear.

everything is hidden from you. you do your rituals and you can feel it all over your skin,

yet you want more. stare into the Eye, it can hear you calling. keep going, keep going, that's the test. if you give up you have to start over. astrology is the game of time, moments written in symbols. the tarot is one translator, symbolism is always the grammar, you are the experiment.

but I want to *be* the all-seeing Eye, the magician's apprentice, the eavesdropper and secret-keeper and she who stands in shadows. show me the way or I will wrestle it from your hold do you want to wrestle with me?

the fantasy is a natural death, the slipping away into blackness, the enveloping Void my eternal lover the one who is there but not there; a restraining hand on my shoulder, an amplification of madness and suffocating negative emotions, anger and hate and ego illumination, frustration and disappointment and waiting,

but I'll wait for you forever because you are the only one. you are the clock ticking in an empty room after midnight, the creeping transformation of young into old, the silent screams and hidden rage and a poker face in the half-light. and, and,

I am a part of you. you know me better than I know myself.

I hide from the others and their saying nothing with many words. I see the way they look at me. my pupils are jittery black holes, all hesitation, infinite knowing bestowed in tiny chunks here and there, spurred on by page turning and distracted meditation, thoughts strewn all over.

The All-Devouring, my love for you is endless suffering. my love for you is that of Stockholm Syndrome, an inherent fear and entrapment, an eventual grudging acceptance of Fate; yet worn like a crown, pride amplified when imagining oneself as Chosen. only we can handle it and thus we are empowered.

show me the way, I look for you wherever I go. how can I talk to the dead, the waiting, those who came before? I want an intimacy others cannot reach. I want to feel you everywhere. I want to be in multiple dimensions at once, out of my body, out of my mind. my love for you is endless suffering, I can't wait to be reunited.

Always yours,
J. Guzmán

if you enjoyed this book

If you enjoyed this book I would love your feedback in the form of a short review. **Your comments are valuable and extremely appreciated, and will help me out on my indie author career path!!**

Follow me on Instagram @jguzmanwriter or visit my website jguzman.space. There you can sign up for my mailing list under the Contact tab.